Lectionary Texts for

Various Occasions and Occasional Services

Together with an
Index to all Lectionary Texts

The Church Hymnal Corporation
800 Second Avenue, New York, New York 10017

The Church Hymnal Corporation desires to express its appreciation to the National Council of Churches for permission to use *The Common Bible*, to the Reverend Terence Lee Wilson for editing this volume, and to Mr. Nelson Gruppo for the layout and design.

The readings have been edited for liturgical use. The opening phrase in many passages is intended to identify the speaker from the outset. For the most part nothing more than a brief phrase of two or three words is needed. In some cases a more extended phrase or clause helps the listener to recall at once to whom the words are addressed and on what occasion. In a few instances, especially when a portion of the reading may be omitted, a brief summary is inserted in italics, to ensure continuity of sense. When the full passage is read, the italicized portion should be omitted. Page references following the citation of Psalms are to the *Book of Common Prayer*. Chapter and verse citations are from *The Common Bible*.

Contents

I
Holy Baptism

Holy Baptism

A Vigil on the Eve of Baptism
[BOS, page 126]

FROM THE OLD TESTAMENT

[The story of the flood]

A Reading (Lesson) from the Book of Genesis
[(7:1-5,11-18);8:6-18;9:8-13]

The Lord said to Noah, "Go into the ark, you and all your household, for I have seen that you are righteous before me in this generation. Take with you seven pairs of all clean animals, the male and his mate; and a pair of the animals that are not clean, the male and his mate; and seven pairs of the birds of the air also, male and female, to keep their kind alive upon the face of all the earth. For in seven days I will send rain upon the earth forty days and forty nights; and every living thing that I have made I will blot out from the face of the ground." And Noah did all that the Lord had commanded him. In the six hundredth year of Noah's life, in the second month, on the seventeenth day of the month, on that day all the fountains of the great deep burst forth, and the windows of the heavens were opened. And rain fell upon the earth forty days and forty nights. On the very same day Noah and his sons, Shem and Ham and Japheth, and Noah's wife and the three wives of his sons with them entered the ark, they and every beast according to its kind, and all the cattle according to their kinds, and every creeping thing that creeps on the earth according to its kind, and every bird according to its kind, every bird of every sort. They went into the ark with Noah, two and two of all flesh in which there was the breath of life. And they that entered, male and female of all flesh, went in as God had commanded him; and the Lord shut him in. The flood continued forty days upon the earth; and the waters increased, and bore up the ark, and it rose high above the earth. The waters prevailed and increased greatly upon the earth; and the ark floated on the face of the waters.

At the end of forty days Noah opened the window of the ark which he had made, and sent forth a raven; and it went to and fro until the waters were dried up from the earth. Then he sent forth a dove from him, to see if the waters had subsided from the face of the ground; but the dove found no place to set her foot, and she returned to him to the ark, for the waters were still on the face of the whole earth. So he put forth his hand and took her and brought her into the ark with him. He waited another seven days, and again he sent forth the dove out of the ark; and the dove came back to him in the evening, and lo, in her mouth a freshly plucked olive leaf; so Noah knew that the waters had subsided from the earth. Then he waited another seven days, and sent forth the dove; and she did not return to him any more. In the six hundred and first year, in the first month, the first day of the month, the waters were dried from off the earth; and Noah removed the covering of the ark, and looked, and behold, the face of the ground was dry. In the second month, on the twenty-seventh day of the month, the earth was dry. Then God said to Noah, "Go forth from the ark, you and your wife, and your sons and your sons' wives with you. Bring forth with you every living thing that is with you of all flesh — birds and animals and every creeping thing that creeps on the earth — that they may breed abundantly on the earth, and be fruitful and multiply upon the earth." Then God said to Noah and to his sons with him, "Behold, I establish my covenant with you and your descendants after you, and with every living creature that is with you, the birds, the cattle, and every beast of the earth with you, as many as came out of the ark. I establish my covenant with you, that never again shall all flesh be cut off by the waters of a flood, and never again shall there be a flood to destroy the earth." And God said, "This is the sign of the covenant which I make between me and you and every living creature that is with you, for all future generations: I set my bow in the cloud, and it shall be a sign of the covenant between me and the earth."

Psalm 25:3-9 [page 614]   or   *Psalm 46* [page 649]

or this

[The story of the covenant]

A Reading (Lesson) from the Book of Exodus
[19:1-9a,16-20a;20:18-20]

On the third new moon after the people of Israel had gone forth out of the land of Egypt, on that day they came into the wilderness of Sinai. And when they set out from Reph'idim and they came into the wilderness of Sinai, they encamped in the wilderness; and there Israel encamped before the mountain. And Moses went up to God, and the Lord called to him out of the mountain, saying, "Thus you shall say to the house of Jacob, and tell the people of

Israel: You have seen what I did to the Egyptians, and how I bore you on eagles' wings and brought you to myself. Now therefore, if you will obey my voice and keep my covenant, you shall be my own possession among all peoples; for all the earth is mine, and you shall be to me a kingdom of priests and a holy nation. These are the words which you shall speak to the children of Israel." So Moses came and called the elders of the people, and set before them all these words which the Lord had commanded him. And all the people answered together and said, "All that the Lord has spoken we will do." And Moses reported the words of the people to the Lord. And the Lord said to Moses, "Lo, I am coming to you in a thick cloud, that the people may hear when I speak with you, and may also believe you for ever." On the morning of the third day there were thunders and lightnings, and a thick cloud upon the mountain, and a very loud trumpet blast, so that all the people who were in the camp trembled. Then Moses brought the people out of the camp to meet God; and they took their stand at the foot of the mountain. And Mount Sinai was wrapped in smoke, because the Lord descended upon it in fire; and the smoke of it went up like the smoke of a kiln, and the whole mountain quaked greatly. And as the sound of the trumpet grew louder and louder, Moses spoke, and God answered him in thunder. And the Lord came down upon Mount Sinai, to the top of the mountain. Now when all the people perceived the thunderings and the lightnings and the sound of the trumpet and the mountain smoking, the people were afraid and trembled; and they stood afar off, and said to Moses, "You speak to us, and we will hear; but let not God speak to us, lest we die." And Moses said to the people, "Do not fear; for God has come to prove you, and that the fear of him may be before your eyes, that you may not sin."

Canticle 2 [page 49]   or   *Canticle 13* [page 90]

or this

[Salvation offered freely to all]

A Reading (Lesson) from the Book of Isaiah [55:1-11]

Thus says the Lord: "Ho, every one who thirsts, come to the waters; and he who has no money, come, buy and eat! Come, buy wine and milk without money and without price. Why do you spend your money for that which is not bread, and your labor for that which does not satisfy? Hearken diligently to me, and eat what is good, and delight yourselves in fatness. Incline your ear, and come to me; hear, that your soul may live; and I will make with you an everlasting covenant, my steadfast, sure love for David. Behold, I made him a witness to the peoples, a leader and commander for the peoples. Behold, you shall call nations that you know not, and nations that knew you not shall run to you, because of the Lord your God, and of the Holy One of Israel, for he has glorified you. Seek the Lord while he may be found, call upon him while he is near; let the wicked forsake his way, and the unrighteous man his thoughts; let him return to the Lord, that he may have mercy on him, and to our God, for he will abundantly pardon. For my thoughts are not your thoughts, neither are your ways my ways, says the Lord. For as the heavens are higher than the earth, so are my ways higher than your ways and my thoughts than your thoughts. For as the rain and the snow come down from heaven, and return not thither but water the earth, making it bring forth and sprout, giving seed to the sower and bread to the eater, so shall my word be that goes forth from my mouth; it shall not return to me empty, but it shall accomplish that which I purpose, and prosper in the thing for which I sent it."

Canticle 9 [page 86]

or this

[A new heart and a new spirit]

A Reading (Lesson) from the Book of Ezekiel
[36:24-28]

Thus says the Lord God: "I will take you from the nations, and gather you from all the countries, and bring you into your own land. I will sprinkle clean water upon you, and you shall be clean from all your uncleannesses, and from all your idols I will cleanse you. A new heart I will give you, and a new spirit I will put within you; and I will take out of your flesh the heart of stone and give you a heart of flesh. And I will put my spirit within you, and cause you to walk in my statutes and be careful to observe my ordinances. You shall dwell in the land which I gave to your fathers; and you shall be my people, and I will be your God."

Psalm 42 [page 643]

or this

[The valley of dry bones]

A Reading (Lesson) from the Book of Ezekiel
[37:1-14]

The hand of the Lord was upon me, and he brought me out by the Spirit of the Lord, and set me down in the midst of the valley; it was full of bones. And he led me round among them; and behold, there were very many upon the valley; and lo, they were very dry. And he said to me, "Son of man, can these bones live?" And I answered, "O Lord God, thou knowest." Again he said to me, "Prophesy to these bones, and say to them, O dry bones, hear the word of the Lord. Thus says the Lord God to these bones: Behold, I will cause breath to enter you, and you shall live. And I will lay sinews upon you, and will cause flesh to come upon you, and cover you with skin, and put breath in you, and you shall live; and you shall know that I am the Lord." So I prophesied as I was commanded; and as I prophesied, there was a noise, and behold, a rattling; and the bones came together, bone to its bone. And as I looked, there were sinews on them, and the flesh had come upon them, and skin had covered them; but there was no breath in them. Then he said to me, "Prophesy to the breath, prophesy, son of man, and say to the breath, Thus says the Lord God: Come from the four winds, O breath, and breathe upon these slain, that they may live." So I prophesied as he commanded me, and the breath came into them, and they lived, and stood upon their feet, an exceedingly great host. Then he said to me, "Son of man, these bones are the whole house of Israel. Behold, they say, 'Our bones are dried up, and our hope is lost; we are clean cut off.' Therefore prophesy, and say to them, Thus says the Lord God: Behold, I will open your graves, and raise you from your graves, O my people; and I will bring you home into the land of Israel. And you shall know that I am the Lord, when I open your graves, and raise you from your graves, O my people. And I will put my Spirit within you, and you shall live, and I will place you in your own land; then you shall know that I, the Lord, have spoken, and I have done it, says the Lord."

Psalm 30 [page 621]   or   *Psalm 143* [page 798]

[Baptized into his death]

*A Reading (Lesson) from the Letter of Paul
to the Romans* [6:3-5]

Do you not know that all of us who have been baptized
into Christ Jesus were baptized into his death? We were
buried therefore with him by baptism into death, so that
as Christ was raised from the dead by the glory of the
Father, we too might walk in newness of life. For if we
have been united with him in a death like his, we shall
certainly be united with him in a resurrection like his.

or this

[We are children of God]

*A Reading (Lesson) from the Letter of Paul
to the Romans* [8:14-17]

All who are led by the Spirit of God are sons of God. For
you did not receive the spirit of slavery to fall back into
fear, but you have received the spirit of sonship. When we
cry, "Abba! Father!" it is the Spirit himself bearing witness
with our spirit that we are children of God, and if
children, then heirs, heirs of God and fellow heirs with
Christ, provided we suffer with him in order that we may
also be glorified with him.

or this

[Now is the day of salvation]

A Reading (Lesson) from the Second Letter of Paul to the Corinthians [5:17-20]

If any one is in Christ, he is a new creation; the old has passed away, behold, the new has come. All this is from God, who through Christ reconciled us to himself and gave us the ministry of reconciliation; that is, in Christ God was reconciling the world to himself, not counting their trespasses against them, and entrusting to us the message of reconciliation. So we are ambassadors for Christ, God making his appeal through us. We beseech you on behalf of Christ, be reconciled to God.

FROM THE HOLY GOSPEL

[The baptism of Jesus]

✝ *The Holy Gospel of Our Lord Jesus Christ According to Mark* [1:1-6]

The beginning of the gospel of Jesus Christ, the Son of God. As it is written in Isaiah the prophet, "Behold, I send my messenger before thy face, who shall prepare thy way; the voice of one crying in the wilderness: Prepare the way of the Lord, make his paths straight —" John the baptizer appeared in the wilderness, preaching a baptism of repentance for the forgiveness of sins. And there went out to him all the country of Judea, and all the people of Jerusalem; and they were baptized by him in the river Jordan, confessing their sins. Now John was clothed with camel's hair, and had a leather girdle around his waist, and ate locusts and wild honey.

or the following

[You must be born again]

✝ *The Holy Gospel of Our Lord Jesus Christ According to John* [3:1-6]

There was a man of the Pharisees, named Nicode'mus, a ruler of the Jews. This man came to Jesus by night and said to him, "Rabbi, we know that you are a teacher come from God; for no one can do these signs that you do, unless God is with him." Jesus answered him, "Truly, truly, I say to you, unless one is born anew, he cannot see the kingdom of God." Nicode'mus said to him, "How can a man be born when he is old? Can he enter a second time into his mother's womb and be born?" Jesus answered, "Truly, truly, I say to you, unless one is born of water and the Spirit, he cannot enter the kingdom of God. That which is born of the flesh is flesh, and that which is born of the Spirit is spirit."

or this

[The resurrection and the great commission]

✝ *The Holy Gospel of Our Lord Jesus Christ According to Matthew* [28:1-10,16-20]

After the sabbath, toward the dawn of the first day of the week, Mary Mag'dalene and the other Mary went to see the sepulchre. And behold, there was a great earthquake; for an angel of the Lord descended from heaven and came and rolled back the stone, and sat upon it. His appearance was like lightning, and his raiment white as snow. And for fear of him the guards trembled and became like dead men. But the angel said to the women, "Do not be afraid; for I know that you seek Jesus who was crucified. He is not here; for he has risen, as he said. Come, see the place where he lay. Then go quickly and tell his disciples that he has risen from the dead, and behold, he is going before you to Galilee; there you will see him. Lo, I have told you." So they departed quickly from the tomb with fear and great joy, and ran to tell his disciples. And behold, Jesus met them and said, "Hail!" And they came up and took hold of his feet and worshiped him. Then Jesus said to them, "Do not be afraid; go and tell my brethren to go to Galilee, and there they will see me." Now the eleven disciples went to Galilee, to the mountain to which Jesus had directed them. And when they saw him they worshiped him; but some doubted. And Jesus came and said to them, "All authority in heaven and on earth has been given to me. Go therefore and make disciples of all nations, baptizing them in the name of the Father and of the Son and of the Holy Spirit, teaching them to observe all that I have commanded you; and lo, I am with you always, to the close of the age."

At Baptism
[BCP, Various Occasions, Proper 10, page 928]

At the principal service on a Sunday or other feast, the Collect and Lessons are properly those of the Day. On other occasions they are selected from the following readings (BCP, rubric, page 300).

When a bishop is present, or on other occasions for sufficient reason, the Collect (page 203 or 254) and one or more of the Lessons provided below may be substituted for the Proper of the Day (Additional Directions, page 212, BCP).

FROM THE OLD TESTAMENT

Ezekiel 36:24-28 [page 14 above]

(Any of the other Old Testament Lessons for the Easter Vigil may be substituted.)

Psalm 15 [page 599] or *Psalm 23* [page 612] or

Psalm 27 [page 617] or *Psalm 42:1-7* [page 643] or

Psalm 84 [page 707] or *Canticle 9* [page 86]

FROM THE NEW TESTAMENT

Romans 6:3-5 [page 16 above] *or this*

Romans 8:14-17 [page 16 above] *or this*

2 Corinthians 5:17-20 [page 17 above]

FROM THE HOLY GOSPEL

✝ *The Holy Gospel of Our Lord Jesus Christ
According to Mark* [1:9-11]

In those days Jesus came from Nazareth of Galilee and
was baptized by John in the Jordan. And when he came up
out of the water, immediately he saw the heavens opened
and the Spirit descending upon him like a dove; and a
voice came from heaven, "Thou art my beloved Son; with
thee I am well pleased."

or this

✝ *The Holy Gospel of Our Lord Jesus Christ
According to Mark* [10:13-16]

They were bringing children to Jesus, that he might touch
them; and the disciples rebuked them. But when Jesus saw
it he was indignant, and said to them, "Let the children
come to me, do not hinder them; for to such belongs the
kingdom of God. Truly, I say to you, whoever does not
receive the kingdom of God like a child shall not enter it."
And he took them in his arms and blessed them, laying his
hands upon them.

or this

John 3:1-6 [page 18 above]

II
Pastoral Offices

Pastoral Offices

At Confirmation

[BCP, Various Occasions, Proper 11, page 929]

At the principal service on a Sunday or other feast, the Collect and Lessons are properly those of the Day. At the discretion of the bishop, however, the Collect (page 203 or 254) and one or more of the Lessons provided below may be substituted. (Rubric on page 414 of BCP.)

FROM THE OLD TESTAMENT

A Reading (Lesson) from the Book of Isaiah [61:1-9]

The Spirit of the Lord God is upon me, because the Lord has anointed me to bring good tidings to the afflicted; he has sent me to bind up the brokenhearted, to proclaim liberty to the captives, and the opening of the prison to those who are bound; to proclaim the year of the Lord's favor, and the day of vengeance of our God; to comfort all those who mourn; to grant to those who mourn in Zion — to give them a garland instead of ashes, the oil of gladness instead of mourning, the mantle of praise instead of a faint spirit; that they may be called oaks of righteousness, the planting of the Lord, that he may be glorified. They shall build up the ancient ruins, they shall raise up the former devastations; they shall repair the ruined cities, the devastations of many generations. Aliens shall stand and feed your flocks, foreigners shall be your plowmen and vinedressers; but you shall be called the priests of the Lord, men shall speak of you as the ministers of our God; you shall eat the wealth of the nations, and in their riches you shall glory. Instead of your shame you shall have a double portion, instead of dishonor you shall rejoice in your lot; therefore in your land you shall possess a double portion; yours shall be everlasting joy. For I the Lord love justice, I hate robbery and wrong; I will faithfully give them their recompense, and I will make an everlasting covenant with them. Their descendants shall be known among the nations, and their offspring in the midst of the peoples; all who see them shall acknowledge them, that they are a people whom the Lord has blessed.

or this

A Reading (Lesson) from the Book of Jeremiah [31:31-34]

Behold, the days are coming, says the Lord, when I will make a new covenant with the house of Israel and the house of Judah, not like the covenant which I made with their fathers when I took them by the hand to bring them out of the land of Egypt, my covenant which they broke, though I was their husband, says the Lord. But this is the covenant which I will make with the house of Israel after those days, says the Lord: I will put my law within them, and I will write it upon their hearts; and I will be their God, and they shall be my people. And no longer shall each man teach his neighbor and each his brother, saying, "Know the Lord," for they shall all know me, from the least of them to the greatest, says the Lord; for I will forgive their iniquity, and I will remember their sin no more.

or this

A Reading (Lesson) from the Book of Ezekiel [37:1-10]

The hand of the Lord was upon me, and he brought me
out by the Spirit of the Lord, and set me down in the midst
of the valley; it was full of bones. And he led me round
among them; and behold there were very many upon the
valley; and lo, they were very dry. And he said to me,
"Son of man, can these bones live?" And I answered, "O
Lord God, thou knowest." Again he said to me, "Prophesy
to these bones, and say to them, O dry bones, hear the
word of the Lord. Thus says the Lord God to these bones:
Behold, I will cause breath to enter you, and you shall live.
And I will lay sinews upon you, and will cause flesh to
come upon you, and cover you with skin, and put breath
in you, and you shall live; and you shall know that I am
the Lord." So I prophesied as I was commanded; and as I
prophesied, there was a noise, and behold, a rattling; and
the bones came together, bone to its bone. And as I
looked, there were sinews on them, and flesh had come
upon them, and skin had covered them; but there was no
breath in them. Then he said to me, "Prophesy to the
breath, prophesy, son of man, and say to the breath, Thus
says the Lord God: Come from the four winds, O breath,
and breathe upon these slain, that they may live." So I
prophesied as he commanded me, and the breath came
into them, and they lived, and stood upon their feet, an
exceedingly great host.

Psalm 1 [page 585]   or   *Psalm 139:1-9* [page 794]

*A Reading (Lesson) from the Letter of Paul
to the Romans* [8:18-27]

I consider that the sufferings of this present time are not
worth comparing with the glory that is to be revealed to
us. For the creation waits with eager longing for the
revealing of the sons of God; for the creation was
subjected to futility, not of its own will but by the will of
him who subjected it in hope; because the creation itself
will be set free from its bondage to decay and obtain the
glorious liberty of the children of God. We know that the
whole creation has been groaning in travail together until
now; and not only the creation, but we ourselves, who
have the first fruits of the Spirit, groan inwardly as we
wait for adoption as sons, the redemption of our bodies.
For in this hope we were saved. Now hope that is seen is
not hope. For who hopes for what he sees? But if we hope
for what we do not see, we wait for it with patience.
Likewise the Spirit helps us in our weakness; for we do not
know how to pray as we ought, but the Spirit himself
intercedes for us with sighs too deep for words. And he
who searches the hearts of men knows what is the mind of
the Spirit, because the Spirit intercedes for the saints
according to the will of God.

or this

*A Reading (Lesson) from the Letter of Paul
to the Romans* [12:1-8]

I appeal to you therefore, brethren, by the mercies of God,
to present your bodies as a living sacrifice, holy and
acceptable to God, which is your spiritual worship. Do
not be conformed to this world but be transformed by the

renewal of your mind, that you may prove what is the will of God, what is good and acceptable and perfect. For by the grace given to me I bid every one among you not to think of himself more highly than he ought to think, but to think with sober judgment, each according to the measure of faith which God has assigned him. For as in one body we have many members, and all the members do not have the same function, so we, though many, are one body in Christ, and individually members one of another. Having gifts that differ according to the grace given to us, let us use them: if prophecy, in proportion to our faith; if service, in our serving; he who teaches, in his teaching; he who exhorts, in his exhortation; he who contributes, in liberality; he who gives aid, with zeal; he who does acts of mercy, with cheerfulness.

or this

A Reading (Lesson) from the Letter of Paul to the Galatians [5:16-25]

I say, walk by the Spirit, and do not gratify the desires of the flesh. For the desires of the flesh are against the Spirit, and the desires of the Spirit are against the flesh; for these are opposed to each other, to prevent you from doing what you would. But if you are led by the Spirit you are not under the law. Now the works of the flesh are plain: fornication, impurity, licentiousness, idolatry, sorcery, enmity, strife, jealousy, anger, selfishness, dissension, party spirit, envy, drunkenness, carousing, and the like. I warn you, as I warned you before, that those who do such things shall not inherit the kingdom of God. But the fruit of the Spirit is love, joy, peace, patience, kindness, goodness, faithfulness, gentleness, self-control; against such there is no law. And those who belong to Christ Jesus have crucified the flesh with its passions and desires. If we live by the Spirit, let us also walk by the Spirit. Let us have no self-conceit, no provoking of one another, no envy of one another.

or this

A Reading (Lesson) from the Letter of Paul to the Ephesians [4:7,11-16]

Grace was given to each of us according to the measure of Christ's gift. And his gifts were that some should be apostles, some prophets, some evangelists, some pastors and teachers, to equip the saints for the work of ministry, for building up the body of Christ, until we all attain to the unity of the faith and of the knowledge of the Son of God, to mature manhood, to the measure of the stature of the fulness of Christ; so that we may no longer be children, tossed to and fro and carried about with every wind of doctrine, by the cunning of men, by their craftiness in deceitful wiles. Rather, speaking the truth in love, we are to grow up in every way into him who is the head, into Christ, from whom the whole body, joined and knit together by every joint with which it is supplied, when each part is working properly, makes bodily growth and upbuilds itself in love.

FROM THE HOLY GOSPEL

✝ *The Holy Gospel of Our Lord Jesus Christ According to Matthew* [5:1-12]

Seeing the crowds, Jesus went up on the mountain, and when he sat down his disciples came to him. And he opened his mouth and taught them, saying: "Blessed are the poor in spirit, for theirs is the kingdom of heaven.

Blessed are those who mourn, for they shall be comforted. Blessed are the meek, for they shall inherit the earth. Blessed are those who hunger and thirst for righteousness, for they shall be satisfied. Blessed are the merciful, for they shall obtain mercy. Blessed are the pure in heart, for they shall see God. Blessed are the peacemakers, for they shall be called sons of God. Blessed are those who are persecuted for righteousness' sake, for theirs is the kingdom of heaven. Blessed are you when men revile you and persecute you and utter all kinds of evil against you falsely on my account. Rejoice and be glad, for your reward is great in heaven, for so men persecuted the prophets who were before you."

or this

✝ *The Holy Gospel of Our Lord Jesus Christ*
According to Matthew [16:24-27]

Jesus told his disciples, "If any man would come after me, let him deny himself and take up his cross and follow me. For whoever would save his life will lose it, and whoever loses his life for my sake will find it. For what will it profit a man, if he gains the whole world and forfeits his life? Or what shall a man give in return for his life? For the Son of man is to come with his angels in the glory of his Father, and then he will repay every man for what he has done."

or this

✝ *The Holy Gospel of Our Lord Jesus Christ*
According to Luke [4:16-21]

Jesus came to Nazareth, where he had been brought up; and he went to the synagogue, as his custom was, on the sabbath day. And he stood up to read; and there was given to him the book of the prophet Isaiah. He opened the book and found the place where it was written, "The Spirit of the Lord is upon me, because he has anointed me to preach good news to the poor. He has sent me to proclaim release to the captives and recovering of sight to the blind, to set at liberty those who are oppressed, to proclaim the acceptable year of the Lord." And he closed the book, and gave it back to the attendant, and sat down; and the eyes of all in the synagogue were fixed on him. And he began to say to them, "Today this scripture has been fulfilled in your hearing."

or this

✝ *The Holy Gospel of Our Lord Jesus Christ According to John* [14:15-21]

Jesus said, "If you love me, you will keep my commandments. And I will pray the Father, and he will give you another Counselor, to be with you for ever, even the Spirit of truth, whom the world cannot receive, because it neither sees him nor knows him; you know him, for he dwells with you, and will be in you. I will not leave you desolate; I will come to you. Yet a little while, and the world will see me no more, but you will see me; because I live, you will live also. In that day you will know that I am in my Father, and you in me, and I in you. He who has my commandments and keeps them, he it is who loves me; and he who loves me will be loved by my Father, and I will love him and manifest myself to him."

At the Celebration and Blessing of a Marriage

[BCP, page 426]

One or more of the following passages from Holy Scripture is read. If there is to be a Communion, a passage from the Gospel always concludes the Readings.

FROM THE OLD TESTAMENT

A Reading (Lesson) from the Book of Genesis [1:26-28]

God said, "Let us make man in our image, after our likeness; and let them have dominion over the fish of the sea, and over the birds of the air, and over the cattle, and over all the earth, and over every creeping thing that creeps upon the earth." So God created man in his own image, in the image of God he created him; male and female he created them. And God blessed them, and God said to them, "Be fruitful and multiply, and fill the earth and subdue it; and have dominion over the fish of the sea and over the birds of the air and over every living thing that moves upon the earth."

or this

A Reading (Lesson) from the Book of Genesis
[2:4-9,15-24]

These are the generations of the heavens and the earth when they were created. In the day that the Lord God made the earth and the heavens, when no plant of the field was yet in the earth and no herb of the field had yet sprung up — for the Lord God had not caused it to rain upon the earth, and there was no man to till the ground; but a mist went up from the earth and watered the whole face of the ground — then the Lord God formed man of dust from the ground, and breathed into his nostrils the breath of life; and man became a living being. And the Lord God planted a garden in Eden, in the east; and there he put the man whom he had formed. And out of the ground the Lord God made to grow every tree that is pleasant to the sight and good for food, the tree of life also in the midst of the garden, and the tree of the knowledge of good and evil. The Lord God took the man and put him in the garden of Eden to till it and keep it. And the Lord God commanded the man, saying, "You may freely eat of every tree of the garden; but of the tree of the knowledge of good and evil you shall not eat, for in the day that you eat of it you shall die." Then the Lord God said, "It is not good that the man should be alone; I will make him a helper fit for him." So out of the ground the Lord God formed every beast of the field and every bird of the air, and brought them to the man to see what he would call them; and whatever the man called every living creature, that was its name. The man gave names to all cattle, and to the birds of the air, and to every beast of the field; but for the man there was not found a helper fit for him. So the Lord God caused a deep sleep to fall upon the man, and while he slept took one of his ribs and closed up its place with flesh; and the rib which the Lord God had taken from the man he made into a woman and brought her to the man. Then the man said, "This at last is bone of my bones and flesh of my flesh; she shall be called Woman, because she was taken out of Man." Therefore a man leaves his father and his mother and cleaves to his wife, and they become one flesh. And the man and his wife were both naked, and were not ashamed.

or this

A Reading (Lesson) from the Song of Solomon
[2:10-13;8:6-7]

My beloved speaks and says to me: "Arise, my love, my fair one, and come away; for lo, the winter is past, the rain is over and gone. The flowers appear on the earth, the time of singing has come, and the voice of the turtledove is heard in our land. The fig tree puts forth its figs, and the vines are in blossom; they give forth fragrance. Arise, my love, my fair one, and come away." Set me as a seal upon your heart, as a seal upon your arm; for love is strong as death, jealousy is cruel as the grave. Its flashes are flashes of fire, a most vehement flame. Many waters cannot quench love, neither can the floods drown it. If a man offered for love all the wealth of his house, it would be utterly scorned.

or this

A Reading (Lesson) from the Book of Tobit
[8:5b-8] *(New English Bible)*

Tobias said to Sarah: "We praise thee, O God of our fathers, we praise thy name for ever and ever. Let the heavens and all thy creation praise thee for ever. Thou madest Adam, and Eve his wife to be his helper and support; and those two were the parents of the human race. This was thy word: 'It is not good for the man to be alone; let us make him a helper like him.' I now take this my beloved to wife, not out of lust but in true marriage. Grant that she and I may find mercy and grow old together." They both said "Amen," and slept through the night.

*A Reading (Lesson) from the First Letter of Paul
to the Corinthians* [13:1-13]

If I speak in the tongues of men and of angels, but have
not love, I am a noisy gong or a clanging cymbal. And if I
have prophetic powers, and understand all mysteries and
all knowledge, and if I have all faith, so as to remove
mountains, but have not love, I am nothing. If I give away
all I have and if I deliver my body to be burned, but have
not love, I gain nothing. Love is patient and kind; love is
not jealous or boastful; it is not arrogant or rude. Love
does not insist on its own way; it is not irritable or
resentful; it does not rejoice at wrong, but rejoices in the
right. Love bears all things, believes all things, hopes all
things, endures all things. Love never ends; as for
prophecies, they will pass away; as for tongues, they will
cease; as for knowledge, it will pass away. For our
knowledge is imperfect and our prophecy is imperfect; but
when the perfect comes, the imperfect will pass away.
When I was a child, I spoke like a child, I thought like a
child, I reasoned like a child; when I became a man, I gave
up childish ways. For now we see in a mirror dimly, but
then face to face. Now I know in part; then I shall
understand fully, even as I have been fully understood. So
faith, hope, love abide, these three; but the greatest of
these is love.

or this

*A Reading (Lesson) from the Letter of Paul
to the Ephesians* [3:14-19]

I bow my knees before the Father, from whom every
family in heaven and on earth is named, that according to

the riches of his glory he may grant you to be strengthened with might through his Spirit in the inner man, and that Christ may dwell in your hearts through faith; that you, being rooted and grounded in love, may have power to comprehend with all the saints what is the breadth and length and height and depth, and to know the love of Christ which surpasses knowledge, that you may be filled with all the fulness of God.

or this

A Reading (Lesson) from the Letter of Paul to the Ephesians [5:1-2,21-33]

Be imitators of God, as beloved children. And walk in love, as Christ loved us and gave himself up for us, a fragrant offering and sacrifice to God. Be subject to one another out of reverence for Christ. Wives, be subject to your husbands, as to the Lord. For the husband is the head of the wife as Christ is the head of the church, his body, and is himself its Savior. As the church is subject to Christ, so let wives also be subject in everything to their husbands. Husbands, love your wives, as Christ loved the church and gave himself up for her, that he might sanctify her, having cleansed her by the washing of water with the word, that he might present the church to himself in splendor, without spot or wrinkle or any such thing, that she might be holy and without blemish. Even so husbands should love their wives as their own bodies. He who loves his wife loves himself. For no man ever hates his own flesh, but nourishes and cherishes it, as Christ does the church, because we are members of his body. "For this reason a man shall leave his father and mother and be joined to his wife, and the two shall become one flesh." This mystery is a profound one, and I am saying that it refers to Christ and the church; however, let each one of you love his wife as himself, and let the wife see that she respects her husband.

or this

A Reading (Lesson) from the Letter of Paul to the Colossians [3:12-17]

Put on then, as God's chosen ones, holy and beloved, compassion, kindness, lowliness, meekness, and patience, forbearing one another and, if one has a complaint against another, forgiving each other; as the Lord has forgiven you, so you also must forgive. And above all these put on love, which binds everything together in perfect harmony. And let the peace of Christ rule in your hearts, to which indeed you were called in the one body. And be thankful. Let the word of Christ dwell in you richly, teach and admonish one another in all wisdom, and sing psalms and hymns and spiritual songs with thankfulness in your hearts to God. And whatever you do, in word or deed, do everything in the name of the Lord Jesus, giving thanks to God the Father through him.

or this

A Reading (Lesson) from the First Letter of John [4:7-16]

Beloved, let us love one another; for love is of God, and he who loves is born of God and knows God. He who does not love does not know God; for God is love. In this the love of God was made manifest among us, that God sent his only Son into the world, so that we might live through him. In this is love, not that we loved God but that he loved us and sent his Son to be the expiation for our sins. Beloved, if God so loved us, we also ought to love one another. No man has ever seen God; if we love one another, God abides in us and his love is perfected in us.

By this we know that we abide in him and he in us, because he has given us of his own Spirit. And we have seen and testify that the Father has sent his Son as the Savior of the world. Whoever confesses that Jesus is the Son of God, God abides in him, and he in God. So we know and believe the love God has for us. God is love, and he who abides in love abides in God, and God abides in him.

Between the Readings, a Psalm, hymn, or anthem may be sung or said. Appropriate Psalms are Psalm 67 [page 675] *or Psalm 127* [page 782] *or Psalm 128* [page 783]

FROM THE HOLY GOSPEL

✠ *The Holy Gospel of Our Lord Jesus Christ According to Matthew* [5:1-10]

Seeing the crowds, Jesus went up on the mountain, and when he sat down his disciples came to him. And he opened his mouth and taught them, saying: "Blessed are the poor in spirit, for theirs is the kingdom of heaven. Blessed are those who mourn, for they shall be comforted. Blessed are the meek, for they shall inherit the earth. Blessed are those who hunger and thirst for righteousness, for they shall be satisfied. Blessed are the merciful, for they shall obtain mercy. Blessed are the pure in heart, for they shall see God. Blessed are the peacemakers, for they shall be called sons of God. Blessed are those who are persecuted for righteousness' sake, for theirs is the kingdom of heaven."

or the following

✝ *The Holy Gospel of Our Lord Jesus Christ
According to Matthew* [5:13-16]

Jesus said, "You are the salt of the earth; but if salt has lost its taste, how shall its saltness be restored? It is no longer good for anything except to be thrown out and trodden under foot by men. You are the light of the world. A city on a hill cannot be hid. Nor do men light a lamp and put it under a bushel, but on a stand, and it gives light to all in the house. Let your light so shine before men, that they may see your good works and give glory to your Father who is in heaven."

or this

✝ *The Holy Gospel of Our Lord Jesus Christ
According to Matthew* [7:21,24-29]

Jesus said, "Not every one who says to me, 'Lord, Lord,' shall enter the kingdom of heaven, but he who does the will of my Father who is in heaven. Every one then who hears these words of mine and does them will be like a wise man who built his house upon the rock; and the rain fell, and the floods came, and the winds blew and beat upon that house, but it did not fall, because it had been founded on the rock. And every one who hears these words of mine and does not do them will be like a foolish man who built his house upon the sand; and the rain fell, and the floods came, and the winds blew and beat against that house, and it fell; and great was the fall of it." And when Jesus finished these sayings, the crowds were astonished at his teaching, for he taught them as one who had authority, and not as their scribes.

or this

✝ *The Holy Gospel of Our Lord Jesus Christ
According to Mark* [10:6-9,13-16]

Jesus said to the Pharisees, "But from the beginning of creation, 'God made them male and female.' 'For this reason a man shall leave his father and mother and be joined to his wife, and the two shall become one flesh.' So they are no longer two but one flesh. What therefore God has joined together, let not man put asunder." And they were bringing children to him, that he might touch them; and the disciples rebuked them. But when Jesus saw it he was indignant, and said to them, "Let the childen come to me, do not hinder them; for to such belongs the kingdom of God. Truly, I say to you, whoever does not receive the kingdom of God like a child shall not enter it." And he took them in his arms and blessed them, laying his hands upon them.

or this

✝ *The Holy Gospel of Our Lord Jesus Christ
According to John* [15:9-12]

Jesus said to his disciples, "As the Father has loved me, so have I loved you; abide in my love. If you keep my commandments, you will abide in my love, just as I have kept my Father's commandments and abide in his love. These things I have spoken to you, that my joy may be in you, and that your joy may be full."

A Thanksgiving for the Birth or Adoption of a Child

[BCP, page 439]

Subject to the rubrics on page 439 of BCP, one of the following may be read:

✝ *The Holy Gospel of Our Lord Jesus Christ According to Luke* [2:41-51]

The parents of Jesus went to Jerusalem every year at the feast of the Passover. And when he was twelve years old, they went up according to custom; and when the feast was ended, as they were returning, the boy Jesus stayed behind in Jerusalem. His parents did not know it, but supposing him to be in the company they went a day's journey, and they sought him among their kinsfolk and acquaintances; and when they did not find him, they returned to Jerusalem, seeking him. After three days they found him in the temple, sitting among the teachers, listening to them and asking them questions; and all who heard him were amazed at his understanding and his answers. And when they saw him they were astonished; and his mother said to him, "Son, why have you treated us so? Behold, your father and I have been looking for you anxiously." And he said to them, "How is it that you sought me? Did you not know that I must be in my Father's house?" And they did not understand the saying which he spoke to them. And he went down with them and came to Nazareth, and was obedient to them; and his mother kept all these things in her heart.

or this

✝ *The Holy Gospel of Our Lord Jesus Christ According to Luke* [18:15-17]

They were bringing even infants to Jesus that he might touch them; and when the disciples saw it, they rebuked them. But Jesus called them to him, saying, "Let the children come to me, and do not hinder them; for to such belongs the kingdom of God. Truly, I say to you, whoever does not receive the kingdom of God like a child shall not enter it."

A Public Service of Healing

[BOS, page 152]

To be used in accordance with the rubrics and suggestions on page 147 of BOS.

FROM THE OLD TESTAMENT

[Manna in the wilderness]

A Reading (Lesson) from the Book of Exodus [16:13-15]

In the evening quails came up and covered the camp; and in the morning dew lay round about the camp. And when the dew had gone up, there was on the face of the wilderness a fine, flake-like thing, fine as hoarfrost on the ground. When the people of Israel saw it, they said to one another, "What is it?" For they did not know what it was. And Moses said to them, "It is the bread which the Lord has given you to eat."

or this

[Eli'jah restores the widow's son to life]

A Reading (Lesson) from the First Book of the Kings
[17:17-24]

The son of the woman, the mistress of the house, became ill; and his illness was so severe that there was no breath left in him. And she said to Eli'jah, "What have you against me, O man of God? You have come to me to bring my sin to remembrance, and to cause the death of my son!" And he said to her, "Give me your son." And he took him from her bosom, and carried him up into the upper chamber, where he lodged, and laid him upon his own bed. And he cried to the Lord, "O Lord my God, hast thou brought calamity even upon the widow with whom I sojourn, by slaying her son?" Then he stretched himself upon the child three times, and cried to the Lord, "O Lord my God, let this child's soul come into him again." And the Lord hearkened to the voice of Eli'jah; and the soul of the child came into him again, and he revived. And Eli'jah took the child, and brought him down from the upper chamber into the house, and delivered him to his mother; and Eli'jah said, "See, your son lives." And the woman said to Eli'jah, "Now I know that you are a man of God, and that the word of the Lord in your mouth is truth."

or this

[Healing of Na'aman]

A Reading (Lesson) from the Second Book of the Kings
[5:9-14]

Na'aman came with his horses and chariots, and halted at

the door of Eli'sha's house. And Eli'sha sent a messenger to him, saying, "Go and wash in the Jordan seven times, and your flesh shall be restored, and you shall be clean." But Na'aman was angry, and went away, saying, "Behold, I thought that he would surely come out to me, and stand, and call on the name of the Lord his God, and wave his hand over the place, and cure the leper. Are not Aba'na and Pharpar, the rivers of Damascus, better than all the waters of Israel? Could I not wash in them, and be clean?" So he turned and went away in a rage. But his servants came near and said to him, "My father, if the prophet had commanded you to do some great thing, would you not have done it? How much rather, then, when he says to you, 'Wash, and be clean'?" So he went down and dipped himself seven times in the Jordan, according to the word of the man of God; and his flesh was restored like the flesh of a little child, and he was clean.

or this

[I have heard your prayer . . . I will heal you]

A Reading (Lesson) from the Second Book of the Kings
[20:1-5]

Hezeki'ah, the son of Ahaz, King of Judah, became sick and was at the point of death. And Isaiah the prophet the son of Amoz came to him, and said to him, "Thus says the Lord, 'Set your house in order; for you shall die, you shall not recover.' " Then Hezeki'ah turned his face to the wall, and prayed to the Lord, saying, "Remember now, O Lord, I beseech thee, how I have walked before thee in faithfulness and with a whole heart, and have done what is good in thy sight." And Hezeki'ah wept bitterly. And before Isaiah had gone out of the middle court, the word of the Lord came to him: "Turn back, and say to

Hezeki'ah the prince of my people, Thus says the Lord, the God of David your father: I have heard your prayer, I have seen your tears; behold, I will heal you; on the third day you shall go up to the house of the Lord."

or this

[The gifts of the Spirit]

A Reading (Lesson) from the Book of Isaiah [11:1-3a]

There shall come forth a shoot from the stump of Jesse, and a branch shall grow out of his roots. And the Spirit of the Lord shall rest upon him, the spirit of wisdom and understanding, the spirit of counsel and might, the spirit of knowledge and the fear of the Lord. And his delight shall be in the fear of the Lord.

or this

[The suffering servant]

A Reading (Lesson) from the Book of Isaiah [42:1-7]

Behold my servant, whom I uphold, my chosen, in whom my soul delights; I have put my Spirit upon him, he will bring forth justice to the nations. He will not cry or lift up his voice, or make it heard in the street; a bruised reed he will not break, and a dimly burning wick he will not quench; he will faithfully bring forth justice. He will not fail or be discouraged till he has established justice in the earth; and the coastlands wait for his law. Thus says God, the Lord, who created the heavens and stretched them out, who spread forth the earth and what comes from it, who gives breath to the people upon it and spirit to those who walk in it: "I am the Lord, I have called you in righteousness, I have taken you by the hand and kept you; I have given you as a covenant to the people, a light to the nations, to open the eyes that are blind, to bring out the prisoners from the dungeon, from the prison those who sit in darkness."

or this

[With his stripes are we healed]

A Reading (Lesson) from the Book of Isaiah [53:3-5]

He was despised and rejected by men; a man of sorrows, and acquainted with grief; and as one from whom men hide their faces he was despised, and we esteemed him not. Surely he has borne our griefs and carried our sorrows; yet we esteemed him stricken, smitten by God, and afflicted. But he was wounded for our transgressions, he was bruised for our iniquities; upon him was the chastisement that made us whole, and with his stripes we are healed.

or this

[Good tidings to the afflicted]

A Reading (Lesson) from the Book of Isaiah [61:1-3]

The Spirit of the Lord God is upon me, because the Lord has anointed me to bring good tidings to the afflicted; he has sent me to bind up the brokenhearted, to proclaim liberty to the captives, and the opening of the prison to those who are bound; to proclaim the year of the Lord's favor, and the day of vengeance of our God; to comfort all who mourn; to grant to those who mourn in Zion — to give them a garland instead of ashes, the oil of gladness instead of mourning, the mantle of praise instead of a faint spirit; that they may be called oaks of righteousness, the planting of the Lord, that he may be glorified.

Psalm 13 [page 597] or *Psalm 20:1-6* [page 608] or

Psalm 23 [page 612] or *Psalm 27* [page 617] or

Psalm 27:1-7, 9, 18 [page 617] or

Psalm 91 [page 719] or *Psalm 103* [page 733] or

Psalm 121 [page 779] or *Psalm 130* [page 784] or

Psalm 139:1-17 [page 794] or

Psalm 145:14-22 [page 801] or *Psalm 146* [page 803]

FROM THE NEW TESTAMENT

[Peter and John heal the lame man]

A Reading (Lesson) from the Acts of the Apostles
[3:1-10]

Now Peter and John were going up to the temple at the hour of prayer, the ninth hour. And a man lame from birth was being carried, whom they laid daily at the gate of the temple which is called Beautiful to ask alms of those who entered the temple. Seeing Peter and John about to go into the temple, he asked for alms. And Peter directed his gaze at him, with John, and said, "Look at us." And he fixed his attention upon them, expecting to receive something from them. But Peter said, "I have no silver and gold, but I give you what I have; in the name of Jesus Christ of Nazareth, walk." And he took him by the right hand and raised him up; and immediately his feet and ankles were made strong. And leaping up he stood and walked and entered the temple with them, walking and leaping and praising God. And all the people saw him walking and praising God, and recognized him as the one who sat for alms at the Beautiful Gate of the temple; and they were filled with wonder and amazement at what had happened to him.

or this

[Healings in Jerusalem; Peter's shadow]

A Reading (Lesson) from the Acts of the Apostles
[5:12-16]

Now many signs and wonders were done among the people by the hands of the apostles. And they were all together in Solomon's Portico. None of the rest dared join them, but the people held them in high honor. And more than ever believers were added to the Lord, multitudes both of men and women, so that they even carried out the sick into the streets, and laid them on beds and pallets, that as Peter came by at least his shadow might fall on some of them. The people also gathered from the towns around Jerusalem, bringing the sick and those afflicted with unclean spirits, and they were all healed.

or this

[Apostolic preaching: He went about . . . healing]

A Reading (Lesson) from the Acts of the Apostles
[10:36-43]

Peter opened his mouth and said: "You know the word which he sent to Israel, preaching good news of peace by Jesus Christ (he is Lord of all), the word which was proclaimed throughout all Judea, beginning from Galilee after the baptism which John preached: how God anointed Jesus of Nazareth with the Holy Spirit and with power; how he went about doing good and healing all that were oppressed by the devil, for God was with him. And we are witnesses to all that he did both in the country of the Jews and in Jerusalem. They put him to death by hanging him on a tree; but God raised him on the third day and made him manifest; not to all the people but to us who were chosen by God as witnesses, who ate and drank with him after he rose from the dead. And he commanded us to preach to the people, and to testify that he is the one ordained by God to be judge of the living and the dead. To him all the prophets bear witness that every one who believes in him receives forgiveness of sins through his name."

or this

[The slave girl with the spirit of divination]

A Reading (Lesson) from the Acts of the Apostles
[16:16-18]

With Paul and Silas, we came to Philippi of Macedo'nia, a Roman colony, and as we were going to the place of prayer, we were met by a slave girl who had a spirit of divination and brought her owners much gain by soothsaying. She followed Paul and us, crying, "These men are servants of the Most High God, who proclaim to you the way of salvation." And this she did for many days. But Paul was annoyed, and turned and said to the spirit, "I charge you in the name of Jesus Christ to come out of her." And it came out that very hour.

or this

[We await the redemption of our bodies]

*A Reading (Lesson) from the Letter of Paul
to the Romans* [8:18-23]

I consider that the sufferings of this present time are not
worth comparing with the glory that is to be revealed to
us. For the creation waits with eager longing for the
revealing of the sons of God; for the creation was
subjected to futility, not of its own will but by the will of
him who subjected it in hope; because the creation itself
will be set free from its bondage to decay and obtain the
glorious liberty of the children of God. We know that the
whole creation has been groaning in travail together until
now; and not only the creation, but we ourselves, who
have the first fruits of the Spirit, groan inwardly as we
wait for adoption as sons, the redemption of our bodies.

or this

[Nothing can separate us from the love of God]

*A Reading (Lesson) from the Letter of Paul
to the Romans* [8:31-39]

What then shall we say to this? If God is for us, who is
against us? He who did not spare his own Son but gave
him up for us all, will he not also give us all things with
him? Who shall bring any charge against God's elect? It is
God who justifies; who is to condemn? Is it Christ Jesus,
who died, yes, who was raised from the dead, who is at
the right hand of God, who indeed intercedes for us? Who
shall separate us from the love of Christ? Shall tribulation,
or distress, or persecution, or famine, or nakedness, or
peril, or sword? As it is written, "For thy sake we are
being killed all the day long; we are regarded as sheep to
be slaughtered." No, in all these things we are more than

conquerors through him who loved us. For I am sure that neither death, nor life, nor angels, nor principalities, nor things present, nor things to come, nor powers, nor height, nor depth, nor anything else in all creation, will be able to separate us from the love of God in Christ Jesus our Lord.

or this

[God comforts us in affliction]

A Reading (Lesson) from the Second Letter of Paul to the Corinthians [1:3-5]

Blessed be the God and Father of our Lord Jesus Christ, the Father of mercies and God of all comfort, who comforts us in all our affliction, so that we may be able to comfort those who are in any affliction, with the comfort with which we ourselves are comforted by God. For as we share abundantly in Christ's sufferings, so through Christ we share abundantly in comfort too.

or this

[May you be strengthened with all power]

A Reading (Lesson) from the Letter of Paul to the Colossians [1:11-20]

May you be strengthened with all power, according to his glorious might, for all endurance and patience with joy, giving thanks to the Father, who has qualified us to share in the inheritance of the saints in light. He has delivered us from the dominion of darkness and transferred us to the kingdom of his beloved Son, in whom we have redemption, the forgiveness of sins. He is the image of the invisible God, the first-born of all creation; for in him all things were created, in heaven and on earth, visible and invisible, whether thrones or dominions or principalities or authorities — all things were created through him and for him. He is before all things, and in him all things hold together. He is the head of the body, the church; he is the beginning, the first-born from the dead, that in everything he might be pre-eminent. For in him all the fulness of God was pleased to dwell, and through him to reconcile to himself all things, whether on earth or in heaven, making peace by the blood of his cross.

or this

[Looking to Jesus, the perfecter of our faith]

A Reading (Lesson) from the Letter to the Hebrews [12:1-2]

Therefore, since we are surrounded by so great a cloud of witnesses, let us also lay aside every weight, and sin which clings so closely, and let us run with perseverance the race that is set before us, looking to Jesus the pioneer and perfecter of our faith, who for the joy that was set before him endured the cross, despising the shame, and is seated at the right hand of the throne of God.

or this

[Is any among you sick?]

A Reading (Lesson) from the Letter of James [5:(13)14-16]

Is any one among you suffering? Let him pray. Is any cheerful? Let him sing praise.

Is any among you sick? Let him call for the elders of the church, and let them pray over him, anointing him with oil in the name of the Lord; and the prayer of faith will save the sick man, and the Lord will raise him up; and if he has committed sins, he will be forgiven. Therefore confess your sins to one another, and pray for one another, that you may be healed. The prayer of a righteous man has great power in its effects.

or this

[That you may know that you have eternal life]

A Reading (Lesson) from the First Letter of John [5:13-15]

I write this to you who believe in the name of the Son of God, that you may know that you have eternal life. And this is the confidence which we have in him, that if we ask anything according to his will he hears us. And if we know that he hears us in whatever we ask, we know that we have obtained the requests made of him.

FROM THE HOLY GOSPEL

[Your sins are forgiven]

✝ *The Holy Gospel of Our Lord Jesus Christ According to Matthew* [9:2-8]

And behold, they brought to Jesus a paralytic, lying on his bed; and when Jesus saw their faith he said to the paralytic, "Take heart, my son; your sins are forgiven." And behold, some of the scribes said to themselves, "This man is blaspheming." But Jesus, knowing their thoughts, said, "Why do you think evil in your hearts? For which is easier, to say, 'Your sins are forgiven,' or to say, 'Rise and walk'? But that you may know that the Son of man has authority on earth to forgive sins" — he then said to the paralytic — "Rise, take up your bed and go home." And he rose and went home. When the crowds saw it, they were afraid, and they glorified God, who had given such authority to men.

or this

[The Last Supper: Not as I will]

✝ *The Holy Gospel of Our Lord Jesus Christ According to Matthew* [26:26-30,36-39]

Now as they were eating, Jesus took bread, and blessed, and broke it, and gave it to the disciples and said, "Take, eat; this is my body." And he took a cup, and when he had given thanks he gave it to them, saying, "Drink of it, all of you; for this is my blood of the covenant, which is poured out for many for the forgiveness of sins. I tell you I shall not drink again of this fruit of the vine until that day when I drink it new with you in my Father's kingdom." Then Jesus went with them to a place called Gethsem'ane, and he said to his disciples, "Sit here, while I go yonder and pray." And taking with him Peter and the two sons of Zeb'edee, he began to be sorrowful and troubled. Then he said to them, "My soul is very sorrowful, even to death; remain here, and watch with me." And going a little farther he fell on his face and prayed, "My Father, if it be possible, let this cup pass from me; nevertheless, not as I will, but as thou wilt."

or the following

[Jesus heals the man with the unclean spirit]

✠ *The Holy Gospel of Our Lord Jesus Christ According to Mark* [1:21-28]

Jesus and his disciples went into Caper'na-um; and immediately on the sabbath he entered the synagogue and taught. And they were astonished at his teaching, for he taught them as one who had authority, and not as the scribes. And immediately there was in their synagogue a man with an unclean spirit; and he cried out, "What have you to do with us, Jesus of Nazareth? Have you come to destroy us? I know who you are, the Holy One of God." But Jesus rebuked him, saying, "Be silent, and come out of him!" And the unclean spirit, convulsing him and crying with a loud voice, came out of him. And they were all amazed, so that they questioned among themselves, saying, "What is this? A new teaching! With authority he commands even the unclean spirits, and they obey him." And at once his fame spread everywhere throughout all the surrounding region of Galilee.

or this

[Jesus heals Peter's mother-in-law and others]

✠ *The Holy Gospel of Our Lord Jesus Christ According to Mark* [1:29-34a]

Jesus left the synagogue at Caper'na-um and entered the house of Simon and Andrew, with James and John. Now Simon's mother-in-law lay sick with a fever, and immediately they told him of her. And he came and took her by the hand and lifted her up, and the fever left her; and she served them. That evening, at sundown, they brought to him all who were sick or possessed with demons. And the whole city was gathered together about the door. And he healed many who were sick with various diseases, and cast out many demons.

or this

[Healing of Ger'asene demoniac]

✝ *The Holy Gospel of Our Lord Jesus Christ According to Mark* [5:1-20]

Jesus and his disciples came to the other side of the sea, to the country of the Ger'asenes. And when he had come out of the boat, there met him out of the tombs a man with an unclean spirit, who lived among the tombs; and no one could bind him any more, even with a chain; for he had often been bound with fetters and chains, but the chains he wrenched apart, and the fetters he broke in pieces; and no one had the strength to subdue him. Night and day he was always crying out, and bruising himself with stones. And when he saw Jesus from afar, he ran and worshiped him; and crying out with a loud voice, he said, "What have you to do with me, Jesus, Son of the Most High God? I adjure you by God, do not torment me." For he had said to him, "Come out of the man, you unclean spirit!" And Jesus asked him, "What is your name?" He replied, "My name is Legion; for we are many." And he begged him eagerly not to send them out of the country. Now a great herd of swine was feeding there on the hillside; and they begged him, "Send us to the swine, let us enter them." So he gave them leave. And the unclean spirits came out, and entered the swine; and the herd, numbering about two thousand, rushed down the steep bank into the sea, and were drowned in the sea. The herdsmen fled, and told it in the city and in the country. And people came to see what it was that had happened. And they came to Jesus, and saw the demoniac sitting there, clothed and in his right mind, the man who had had the legion; and they were afraid. And those who had seen it told what had happened to the demoniac and to the swine. And they began to beg Jesus to depart from their neighborhood. And as he was getting into the boat, the man who had been possessed with demons begged him that he might be with him. But he refused, and said to him, "Go home to your friends, and tell them how much the Lord has done for you, and how he has had mercy on you." And he went away and began to proclaim in the Decap'olis how much Jesus had done for him; and all men marveled.

or this

[Healing of Ja'irus' daughter]

✝ *The Holy Gospel of Our Lord Jesus Christ According to Mark* [5:22-24]

Then came one of the rulers of the synagogue, Ja'irus by name; and seeing Jesus, he fell at his feet, and besought him, saying, "My little daughter is at the point of death. Come and lay your hands on her, so that she may be made well, and live." And he went with him.

or this

[They anointed with oil many that were sick]

✝ *The Holy Gospel of Our Lord Jesus Christ According to Mark* [6:7,12-13]

Jesus called to him the twelve, and began to send them out two by two, and gave them authority over the unclean spirits. So they went out and preached that men should repent. And they cast out many demons, and anointed with oil many that were sick and healed them.

or this

[Your faith has made you well]

✝ *The Holy Gospel of Our Lord Jesus Christ According to Luke* [17:11-19]

On the way to Jerusalem Jesus was passing along between Samar'ia and Galilee. And as he entered a village, he was met by ten lepers, who stood at a distance and lifted up their voices and said, "Jesus, Master, have mercy on us." When he saw them he said to them, "Go and show yourselves to the priests." And as they went they were cleansed. Then one of them, when he saw that he was healed, turned back, praising God with a loud voice; and he fell on his face at Jesus' feet, giving him thanks. Now he was a Samaritan. Then said Jesus, "Were not ten cleansed? Where are the nine? Was no one found to return and give praise to God except this foreigner?" And he said to him, "Rise and go your way; your faith has made you well."

or this

[Do you want to be healed?]

✝ *The Holy Gospel of Our Lord Jesus Christ According to John* [5:1b-9]

Jesus went up to Jerusalem. Now there is in Jerusalem by the Sheep Gate a pool, in Hebrew called Beth-za'tha, which has five porticoes. In these lay a multitude of invalids, blind, lame, paralyzed. One man was there, who

had been ill for thirty-eight years. When Jesus saw him
and knew that he had been lying there a long time, he said
to him, "Do you want to be healed?" The sick man
answered him, "Sir, I have no man to put me into the pool
when the water is troubled, and while I am going another
steps down before me." Jesus said to him, "Rise, take up
your pallet, and walk." And at once the man was healed,
and he took up his pallet and walked.

or this

[I am the bread of life]

✝ *The Holy Gospel of Our Lord Jesus Christ
According to John* [6:47-51]

Jesus said to the people, "Truly, truly, I say to you, he who
believes has eternal life. I am the bread of life. Your fathers
ate the manna in the wilderness, and they died. This is the
bread which comes down from heaven, that a man may
eat of it and not die. I am the living bread which came
down from heaven; if any one eats of this bread, he will
live for ever; and the bread which I shall give for the life of
the world is my flesh."

or this

[Healing of the man born blind]

✝ *The Holy Gospel of Our Lord Jesus Christ
According to John* [9:1-11]

As Jesus passed by, he saw a man blind from his birth. And
his disciples asked him, "Rabbi, who sinned, this man or
his parents, that he was born blind?" Jesus answered,
"It was not that this man sinned, or his parents, but that

the works of God might be made manifest in him. We must work the works of him who sent me, while it is day; night comes, when no one can work. As long as I am in the world, I am the light of the world." As he said this, he spat on the ground and made clay of the spittle and anointed the man's eyes with the clay, saying to him, "Go, wash in the pool of Silo'am" (which means Sent). So he went and washed and came back seeing. The neighbors and those who had seen him before as a beggar, said, "Is not this the man who used to sit and beg?" Some said, "It is he"; others said, "No, but he is like him." He said, "I am the man." They said to him, "Then how were your eyes opened?" He answered, "The man called Jesus made clay and anointed my eyes and said to me, 'Go to Silo'am and wash'; so I went and washed and received my sight."

Ministration to the Sick
[BCP, page 453]

General

A Reading (Lesson) from the Second Letter of Paul to the Corinthians [1:3-5]

Blessed be the God and Father of our Lord Jesus Christ, the Father of mercies and God of all comfort, who comforts us in all our affliction, so that we may be able to comfort those who are in any affliction, with the comfort with which we ourselves are comforted by God. For as we share abundantly in Christ's sufferings, so through Christ we share abundantly in comfort too.

Psalm 91 [page 719]

Luke 17:11-19 [page 59 above]

Penitence

Hebrews 12:1-2 [page 53 above]

Psalm 103 [page 733]

Matthew 9:2-8 [page 54 above]

When Anointing is to follow

A Reading (Lesson) from the Letter of James [5:14-16]

Is any among you sick? Let him call for the elders of the church, and let them pray over him, anointing him with oil in the name of the Lord; and the prayer of faith will save the sick man, and the Lord will raise him up; and if he has committed sins, he will be forgiven. Therefore confess yours sins to one another, and pray for one another, that you may be healed. The prayer of a righteous man has great power in its effects.

Psalm 23 [page 612]

Mark 6:7, 12-13 [page 58 above]

When Communion is to follow

1 John 5:13-15 [page 54 above]

Psalm 145:14-22 [page 802]

John 6:47-51 [page 60 above]

For the Sick
[BCP, Various Occasions, Proper 20, page 931]

A Reading (Lesson) from the Second Book of the Kings [20:1-5]

Hezeki'ah, the son of Ahaz, King of Judah, became sick and was at the point of death. And Isaiah the prophet the son of Amoz came to him, and said to him, "Thus says the Lord, 'Set your house in order; for you shall die, you shall not recover,' " Then Hezeki'ah turned his face to the wall, and prayed to the Lord, saying, "Remember now, O Lord, I beseech thee, how I have walked before thee in faithfulness and with a whole heart, and have done what is good in thy sight." And Hezeki'ah wept bitterly. And before Isaiah had gone out of the middle court, the word of the Lord came to him: "Turn back, and say to Hezeki'ah the prince of my people, Thus says the Lord, the God of David your father: I have heard your prayer, I have seen your tears; behold, I will heal you; on the third day you shall go up to the house of the Lord."

Psalm 13 [page 597] or *Psalm 86:1-7* [page 709]

A Reading (Lesson) from the Letter of James [5:13-16]

Is any one among you suffering? Let him pray. Is any cheerful? Let him sing praise. Is any among you sick? Let him call for the elders of the church, and let them pray over him, anointing him with oil in the name of the Lord; and the prayer of faith will save the sick man, and the Lord will raise him up; and if he has committed sins, he will be forgiven. Therefore confess your sins to one another, and pray for one another, that you may be healed. The prayer of a righteous man has great power in its effects.

✝ *The Holy Gospel of Our Lord Jesus Christ According to Mark* [2:1-12]

When Jesus returned to Caper'na-um after some days, it was reported that he was at home. And many were gathered together, so that there was no longer room for them, not even about the door; and he was preaching the word to them. And they came, bringing to him a paralytic carried by four men. And when they could not get near him because of the crowd, they removed the roof above him; and when they had made an opening, they let down the pallet on which the paralytic lay. And when Jesus saw their faith, he said to the paralytic, "My son, your sins are forgiven." Now some of the scribes were sitting there, questioning in their hearts, "Why does this man speak thus? It is blasphemy! Who can forgive sins but God alone?" And immediately Jesus, perceiving in his spirit that they thus questioned within themselves, said to them, "Why do you question thus in your hearts? Which is easier, to say to the paralytic, 'Your sins are forgiven,' or to say, 'Rise, take up your pallet and walk'? But that you may know that the Son of man has authority on earth to forgive sins" — he said to the paralytic — "I say to you, rise, take up your pallet and go home." And he rose, and immediately took up the pallet and went out before them all; so that they were all amazed and glorified God, saying, "We never saw anything like this!"

Any of the Psalms and Lessons appointed at the Ministration to the Sick (page 62 above) may be used instead.

At the Burial of the Dead

[BCP, pages 470, 494]

Subject to the rubrics, one or more of the following passages from Holy Scripture is read.

FROM THE OLD TESTAMENT

ᵛ 1

[He will swallow up death for ever]

A Reading (Lesson) from the Book of Isaiah [25:6-9]

On this mountain the Lord of hosts will make for all peoples a feast of fat things, a feast of wine on the lees, of fat things full of marrow, of wine on the lees well refined. And he will destroy on this mountain the covering that is cast over all peoples, the veil that is spread over all nations. He will swallow up death for ever, and the Lord God will wipe away tears from all faces, and the reproach of his people he will take away from all the earth; for the Lord has spoken. It will be said on that day, "Lo, this is our God; we have waited for him, that he might save us. This is the Lord; we have waited for him; let us be glad and rejoice in his salvation."

or this

[To comfort those who mourn]

A Reading (Lesson) from the Book of Isaiah [61:1-3]

The Spirit of the Lord God is upon me, because the Lord has anointed me to bring good tidings to the afflicted; he has sent me to bind up the brokenhearted, to proclaim liberty to the captives, and the opening of the prison to those who are bound; to proclaim the year of the Lord's favor, and the day of vengeance of our God; to comfort all who mourn; to grant to those who mourn in Zion — to give them a garland instead of ashes, the oil of gladness instead of mourning, the mantle of praise instead of a faint spirit; that they may be called oaks of righteousness, the planting of the Lord, that he may be glorified.

or this

[The Lord is good to those who wait for him]

A Reading (Lesson) from the Book of Lamentations [3:22-26,31-33]

The steadfast love of the Lord never ceases, his mercies never come to an end; they are new every morning; great is thy faithfulness. "The Lord is my portion," says my soul, "therefore I will hope in him." The Lord is good to those who wait for him, to the soul that seeks him. It is good that one should wait quietly for the salvation of the Lord. For the Lord will not cast off for ever, but, though he cause grief, he will have compassion according to the abundance of his steadfast love; for he does not willingly afflict or grieve the sons of men.

or this

[The souls of the righteous are in the hand of God]

A Reading (Lesson) from the Book of Wisdom [3:1-5,9]

The souls of the righteous are in the hand of God, and no torment will ever touch them. In the eyes of the foolish they seemed to have died, and their departure was thought to be an affliction, and their going from us to be their destruction; but they are at peace. For though in the sight of men they were punished, their hope is full of immortality. Having been disciplined a little, they will receive great good, because God tested them and found them worthy of himself. Those who trust in him will understand truth, and the faithful will abide with him in love, because grace and mercy are upon his elect, and he watches over his holy ones.

or this

[I know that my Redeemer lives]

A Reading (Lesson) from the Book of Job [19:21-27a]

Job answered, "Have pity on me, have pity on me, O you my friends, for the hand of God has touched me! Why do you, like God, pursue me? Why are you not satisfied with my flesh? Oh that my words were written! Oh that they were inscribed in a book! Oh that with an iron pen and lead they were graven in the rock for ever! For I know that my Redeemer lives, and at last he will stand upon the earth; and after my skin has been thus destroyed, then from my flesh I shall see God, whom I shall see on my side, and my eyes shall behold, and not another."

A suitable psalm, hymn, or canticle may follow. The following psalms are appropriate: Psalm 42:1-7 [page 643] or *Psalm 46* [page 649] or *Psalm 90:1-12* [page 717] or *Psalm 121* [page 779] or *Psalm 130* [page 784] or *Psalm 139:1-11* [page 794].

FROM THE NEW TESTAMENT

[The glory that shall be revealed]

A Reading (Lesson) from the Letter of Paul to the Romans [8:14-19,34-35,37-39]

All who are led by the Spirit of God are sons of God. For you did not receive the spirit of slavery to fall back into fear, but you have received the spirit of sonship. When we cry, "Abba! Father!" it is the Spirit himself bearing witness with our spirit that we are children of God, and if children, then heirs, heirs of God and fellow heirs with Christ, provided we suffer with him in order that we may also be glorified with him. I consider that the sufferings of this present time are not worth comparing with the glory that is to be revealed to us. For the creation waits with eager longing for the revealing of the sons of God. Who is to condemn? Is it Christ Jesus, who died, yes, who was raised from the dead, who is at the right hand of God, who indeed intercedes for us? Who shall separate us from the love of Christ? Shall tribulation, or distress, or persecution, or famine, or nakedness, or peril, or sword? No, in all these things we are more than conquerors through him who loved us. For I am sure that neither death, nor life, nor angels, nor principalities, nor things present, nor things to come, nor powers, nor height, nor depth, nor anything else in all creation, will be able to separate us from the love of God in Christ Jesus our Lord.

or this

[The imperishable body]

A Reading (Lesson) from the First Letter of Paul to the Corinthians [15:20-26,35-38,42-44,53-58]

In fact Christ has been raised from the dead, the first fruits of those who have fallen asleep. For as by a man came death, by a man has come also the resurrection of the dead. For as in Adam all die, so also in Christ shall all be made alive. But each in his own order: Christ the first fruits, then at his coming those who belong to Christ. Then comes the end, when he delivers the kingdom to God the Father after destroying every rule and every authority and power. For he must reign until he has put all his enemies under his feet. The last enemy to be destroyed is death. But some one will ask, "How are the dead raised? With what kind of body do they come?" You foolish man! What you sow does not come to life unless it dies. And what you sow is not the body which is to be, but a bare kernel, perhaps of wheat or of some other grain. But God gives it a body as he has chosen, and to each kind of seed its own body. So is it with the resurrection of the dead. What is sown is perishable, what is raised is imperishable. It is sown in dishonor, it is raised in glory. It is sown in weakness, it is raised in power. It is sown a physical body, it is raised a spiritual body. If there is a physical body, there is also a spiritual body. For this perishable nature must put on the imperishable, and this mortal nature must put on immortality. When the perishable puts on the imperishable, and the mortal puts on immortality, then shall come to pass the saying that is written: "Death is swallowed up in victory." "O death, where is thy victory? O death, where is thy sting?" The sting of death is sin, and the power of sin is the law. But thanks be to God, who gives us the victory through our Lord Jesus Christ. Therefore, my beloved brethren, be steadfast, immovable, always abounding in the work of the Lord, knowing that in the Lord your labor is not in vain.

or this

[Things that are unseen are eternal]

A Reading (Lesson) from the Second Letter of Paul to the Corinthians [4:16—5:9]

We do not lose heart. Though our outer nature is wasting away, our inner nature is being renewed every day. For this slight momentary affliction is preparing for us an eternal weight of glory beyond all comparison, because we look not to the things that are seen but to the things that are unseen; for things that are seen are transient, but the things that are unseen are eternal. For we know that if the earthly tent we live in is destroyed, we have a building from God, a house not made with hands, eternal in the heavens. Here indeed we groan, and long to put on our heavenly dwelling, so that by putting it on we may not be found naked. For while we are still in this tent, we sigh with anxiety; not that we would be unclothed, but that we would be further clothed, so that what is mortal may be swallowed up by life. He who has prepared us for this very thing is God, who has given us the Spirit as a guarantee. So we are always of good courage; we know that while we are at home in the body we are away from the Lord, for we walk by faith, not by sight. We are of good courage, and we would rather be away from the body and at home with the Lord. So whether we are at home or away, we make it our aim to please him.

or this

[We shall be like him]

A Reading (Lesson) from the First Letter of John [3:1-2]

See what love the Father has given us, that we should be called children of God; and so we are. The reason why the world does not know us is that it did not know him. Beloved, we are God's children now; it does not yet appear what we shall be, but we know that when he appears we shall be like him, for we shall see him as he is.

or this

[God will wipe away every tear]

A Reading (Lesson) from the Revelation to John [7:9-17]

After this I looked, and behold, a great multitude which no man could number, from every nation, from all tribes and peoples and tongues, standing before the throne and before the Lamb, clothed in white robes, with palm branches in their hands, and crying out with a loud voice, "Salvation belongs to our God who sits upon the throne, and to the Lamb!" And all the angels stood round the throne and round the elders and the four living creatures, and they fell on their faces before the throne and worshiped God, saying, "Amen! Blessing and glory and wisdom and thanksgiving and honor and power and might be to our God for ever and ever! Amen!" Then one of the elders addressed me, saying, "Who are these, clothed in white robes, and whence have they come?" I said to him, "Sir, you know." And he said to me, "These are they who have come out of the great tribulation; they have washed their robes and made them white in the blood of the Lamb. Therefore are they before the throne of God, and serve him day and night within his temple; and he who sits upon the throne will shelter them with his presence. They shall hunger no more, neither thirst any more; the sun shall not strike them, nor any scorching heat. For the Lamb in the midst of the throne will be their shepherd, and he will guide them to springs of living water; and God will wipe away every tear from their eyes."

or this

[Behold, I make all things new]

A Reading (Lesson) from the Revelation to John [21:2-7]

I saw the holy city, new Jerusalem, coming down out of heaven from God, prepared as a bride adorned for her husband; and I heard a loud voice from the throne saying, "Behold, the dwelling of God is with men. He will dwell with them, and they shall be his people, and God himself will be with them; he will wipe away every tear from their eyes, and death shall be no more, neither shall there be mourning nor crying nor pain any more, for the former things have passed away." And he who sat upon the throne said, "Behold, I make all things new." Also he said, "Write this, for these words are trustworthy and true." And he said to me, "It is done! I am the Alpha and the Omega, the beginning and the end. To the thirsty I will give from the fountain of the water of life without payment. He who conquers shall have this heritage, and I will be his God and he shall be my son."

A suitable psalm, hymn, or canticle may follow. The following psalms are appropriate: Psalm 23 [page 612] or *Psalm 27* [page 617] or *Psalm 106:1-5* [page 741] or *Psalm 116* [page 759].

FROM THE HOLY GOSPEL

[He who believes has everlasting life]

✝ *The Holy Gospel of Our Lord Jesus Christ According to John* [5:24-27]

Jesus said to the people, "Truly, truly, I say to you, he who hears my word and believes him who sent me, has eternal life; he does not come into judgment, but has passed from death to life. Truly, truly, I say to you, the hour is coming, and now is, when the dead will hear the voice of the Son of God, and those who hear will live. For as the Father has life in himself, so he has granted the Son also to have life in himself, and has given him authority to execute judgment, because he is the Son of man."

or this

[All that the Father gives me will come to me]

✝ *The Holy Gospel of Our Lord Jesus Christ According to John* [6:37-40]

Jesus said to the people, "All that the Father gives me will come to me; and him who comes to me I will not cast out.

For I have come down from heaven, not to do my own will, but the will of him who sent me, that I should lose nothing of all that he has given me, but raise it up at the last day. For this is the will of my Father, that every one who sees the Son and believes in him should have eternal life; and I will raise him up at the last day."

or this

[I am the good shepherd]

✝ *The Holy Gospel of Our Lord Jesus Christ According to John* [10:11-16]

Jesus said, "I am the good shepherd. The good shepherd lays down his life for the sheep. He who is a hireling and not a shepherd, whose own the sheep are not, sees the wolf coming and leaves the sheep and flees; and the wolf snatches them and scatters them. He flees because he is a hireling and cares nothing for the sheep. I am the good shepherd; I know my own and my own know me, as the Father knows me and I know the Father; and I lay down my life for the sheep. And I have other sheep, that are not of this fold; I must bring them also, and they will heed my voice. So there shall be one flock, one shepherd."

or this

[I am the resurrection and the life]

✝ *The Holy Gospel of Our Lord Jesus Christ According to John* [11:21-27]

Martha said to Jesus, "Lord, if you had been here, my brother would not have died. And even now I know that whatever you ask from God, God will give you." Jesus said to her, "Your brother will rise again." Martha said to him, "I know that he will rise again in the resurrection at the last day." Jesus said to her, "I am the resurrection and the life; he who believes in me, though he die, yet shall he live, and whoever lives and believes in me shall never die. Do you believe this?" She said to him, "Yes, Lord; I believe that you are the Christ, the Son of God, he who is coming into the world."

or this

[In my Father's house are many rooms]

✝ *The Holy Gospel of Our Lord Jesus Christ According to John* [14:1-6]

Jesus said, "Let not your hearts be troubled; believe in God, believe also in me. In my Father's house are many rooms; if it were not so, would I have told you that I go to prepare a place for you? And when I go and prepare a place for you, I will come again and will take you to myself, that where I am you may be also. And you know the way where I am going." Thomas said to him, "Lord, we do not know where you are going; how can we know the way?" Jesus said to him, "I am the way, and the truth, and the life; no one comes to the Father, but by me."

For the Departed

[BCP, Various Occasions, Proper 8, page 928]

FROM THE OLD TESTAMENT

Isaiah 25:6-9 [page 65 above]

or this

A Reading (Lesson) from the Book of Wisdom [3:1-9]

The souls of the righteous are in the hand of God, and no torment will ever touch them. In the eyes of the foolish they seemed to have died, and their departure was thought to be an affliction, and their going from us to be their destruction; but they are at peace. For though in the sight of men they were punished, their hope is full of immortality. Having been disciplined a little, they will receive great good, because God tested them and found them worthy of himself; like gold in the furnace he tried them, and like a sacrificial burnt offering he accepted them. In the time of their visitation they will shine forth, and will run like sparks through the stubble. They will govern nations and rule over peoples, and the Lord will reign over them for ever. Those who trust in him will understand truth, and the faithful will abide with him in love, because grace and mercy are upon his elect, and he watches over his holy ones.

Psalm 116 [page 759]   or

Psalm 103:13-22 [page 734]   or

Psalm 130 [page 784]

FROM THE NEW TESTAMENT

*A Reading (Lesson) from the First Letter of Paul
to the Corinthians* [15:50-58]

I tell you this, brethren: flesh and blood cannot inherit the
kingdom of God, nor does the perishable inherit the
imperishable. Lo! I tell you a mystery. We shall not all
sleep, but we shall all be changed, in a moment, in the
twinkling of an eye, at the last trumpet. For the trumpet
will sound, and the dead will be raised imperishable, and
we shall be changed. For this perishable nature must put
on the imperishable, and this mortal nature must put on
immortality, then shall come to pass the saying that is
written: "Death is swallowed up in victory." "O death,
where is thy victory? O death, where is thy sting?" The
sting of death is sin, and the power of sin is the law. But
thanks be to God, who gives us the victory through our
Lord Jesus Christ. Therefore, my beloved brethren, be
steadfast, immovable, always abounding in the work of
the Lord, knowing that in the Lord your labor is not in
vain.

FROM THE HOLY GOSPEL

John 5:24-27 [page 73 above]

or this

John 6:37-40 [page 73 above]

or this

John 11:21-27 [page 74 above]

*Any of the Psalms and Lessons appointed at the Burial of the Dead
(page 65 above) may be used instead.*

For All Faithful Departed

[November 2, LFF, page 365]

FROM THE OLD TESTAMENT

A Reading (Lesson) from the Book of Wisdom [3:1-9]

The souls of the righteous are in the hand of God, and no torment will ever touch them. In the eyes of the foolish they seemed to have died, and their departure was thought to be an affliction, and their going from us to be their destruction; but they are at peace. For though in the sight of men they were punished, their hope is full of immortality. Having been disciplined a little, they will receive great good, because God tested them and found them worthy of himself; like gold in the furnace he tried them, and like a sacrificial burnt offering he accepted them. In the time of their visitation they will shine forth, and will run like sparks through the stubble. They will govern nations and rule over peoples, and the Lord will reign over them for ever. Those who trust in him will understand truth, and the faithful will abide with him in love, because grace and mercy are upon his elect, and he watches over his holy ones.

or this

A Reading (Lesson) from the Book of Isaiah [25:6-9]

On this mountain the Lord of hosts will make for all peoples a feast of fat things, a feast of wine on the lees, of fat things full of marrow, of wine on the lees well refined. And he will destroy on this mountain the covering that is cast over all peoples, the veil that is spread over all nations.

He will swallow up death for ever, and the Lord God will wipe away tears from all faces, and the reproach of his people he will take away from all the earth; for the Lord has spoken. It will be said on that day, "Lo, this is our God; we have waited for him, that he might save us. This is the Lord; we have waited for him; let us be glad and rejoice in his salvation."

Psalm 130 [page 784]   or   *Psalm 116:10-17* [page 759]

FROM THE NEW TESTAMENT

A Reading (Lesson) from the First Letter of Paul to the Thessalonians [4:13-18]

We would not have you ignorant, brethren, concerning those who are asleep, that you may not grieve as others do who have no hope. For since we believe that Jesus died and rose again, even so, through Jesus, God will bring with him those who have fallen asleep. For this we declare to you by the word of the Lord, that we who are alive, who are left until the coming of the Lord, shall not precede those who have fallen asleep. For the Lord himself will descend from heaven with a cry of command, with the archangel's call, and with the sound of the trumpet of God. And the dead in Christ will rise first; then we who are alive, who are left, shall be caught up together with them in the clouds to meet the Lord in the air; and so we shall always be with the Lord. Therefore comfort one another with these words.

or this

1 Corinthians 15:50-58 [page 77 above]

FROM THE HOLY GOSPEL

✝ *The Holy Gospel of Our Lord Jesus Christ*
According to John [5:24-27]

Jesus said to the people, "Truly, truly, I say to you, he who hears my word and believes him who sent me, has eternal life; he does not come into judgment, but has passed from death to life. Truly, truly, I say to you, the hour is coming, and now is, when the dead will hear the voice of the Son of God, and those who hear will live. For as the Father has life in himself, so he has granted the Son also to have life in himself, and has given him authority to execute judgment, because he is the Son of man."

Burial of One Who does not Profess the Christian Faith

[BOS, page 156]

The anthem, and any of the following Psalms, Lessons, with the Prayers on pages 157-9, and the form of Committal may be used with the Order for Burial on page 506 of the Prayer Book.

FROM THE OLD TESTAMENT

[For everything there is a season]

A Reading (Lesson) from the Book of Ecclesiastes [3:1-11]

For everything there is a season, and a time for every matter under heaven: a time to be born, and a time to die; a time to plant, and a time to pluck up what is planted; a time to kill, and a time to heal; a time to break down, and a time to build up; a time to weep, and a time to laugh; a time to mourn, and a time to dance; a time to cast away stones, and a time to gather stones together; a time to embrace, and a time to refrain from embracing; a time to seek, and a time to lose; a time to keep, and a time to cast away; a time to rend, and a time to sew; a time to keep silence, and a time to speak; a time to love, and a time to hate; a time for war, and a time for peace. What gain has the worker from his toil? I have seen the business that God has given to the sons of men to be busy with. He has made everything beautiful in its time; also he has put eternity into a man's mind, yet so that he cannot find out what God has done from the beginning to the end.

or this

[Remember your Creator in the days of your youth]

A Reading (Lesson) from the Book of Ecclesiastes
[12:1-7]

Remember your Creator in the days of your youth, before the evil days come, and the years draw nigh, when you will say, "I have no pleasure in them"; before the sun and the light and the moon and the stars are darkened and the clouds return after the rain; in the day when the keepers of the house tremble, and the strong men are bent, and the grinders cease because they are few, and those that look through the windows are dimmed, and the doors on the street are shut; when the sound of the grinding is low, and one rises up at the voice of a bird, and all the daughters of song are brought low; they are afraid also of what is high, and terrors are in the way; the almond tree blossoms, the grasshopper drags itself along and desire fails; because man goes to his eternal home, and the mourners go about the streets; before the silver cord is snapped, or the golden bowl is broken, or the pitcher is broken at the fountain, or the wheel broken at the cistern, and the dust returns to the earth as it was, and the spirit returns to God who gave it.

Psalm 23 [page 612] or *Psalm 90* [page 717] or

Psalm 121 [page 779] or *Psalm 130* [page 784]

FROM THE NEW TESTAMENT

[Who shall separate us from the love of Christ?]

A Reading (Lesson) from the Letter of Paul to the Romans [8:35-39]

Who shall separate us from the love of Christ? Shall tribulation, or distress, or persecution, or famine, or nakedness, or peril, or sword? As it is written, "For thy sake we are being killed all the day long; we are regarded as sheep to be slaughtered." No, in all these things we are more than conquerors through him who loved us. For I am sure that neither death, nor life, nor angels, nor principalities, nor things present, nor things to come, nor powers, nor height, nor depth, nor anything else in all creation, will be able to separate us from the love of God in Christ Jesus our Lord.

FROM THE HOLY GOSPEL

[I am the good shepherd]

John 10:11-16 [page 74 above]

III
The Church Year

The Church Year

Advent Festival of Lessons and Music
[BOS, page 32]

FROM THE OLD TESTAMENT

[God creates man and woman to live in obedience to him in the Garden of Eden]

A Reading (Lesson) from the Book of Genesis [2:4b-9,15-25]

In the day that the Lord God made the earth and the heaven, when no plant of the field had yet sprung up—for the Lord God had not caused it to rain upon the earth, and there was no man to till the ground; but a mist went up from the earth and watered the whole face of the ground—then the Lord God formed man of dust from the ground, and breathed into his nostrils the breath of life; and man became a living being. And the Lord God planted a garden in Eden, in the east; and there he put the man whom he had formed. And out of the ground the Lord God made to grow every tree that is pleasant to the sight and good for food, the tree of life also in the midst of the garden and the tree of the knowledge of good and evil. The Lord God took the man and put him in the garden of Eden to till it and keep it. And the Lord God commanded the man, saying, "You may freely eat of every tree of the garden; but of the tree of the knowledge of good and evil you shall not eat, for in the day that you eat of it you shall die." Then the Lord God said, "It is not good that the man should be alone; I will make him a helper fit for him." So out of the ground the Lord God formed every beast of the field and every bird of the air, and brought them to the man to see what he would call them; and whatever the man called every living creature, that was its name. The man gave names to all cattle, and to the birds of the air, and to every beast of the field; but for the man there was not found a helper fit for him. So the Lord God caused a deep sleep to fall upon the man, and while he slept took one of his ribs and closed up its place with flesh; and the rib which the Lord God had taken from the man he made into a woman and brought her to the man. Then the man said, "This at last is bone of my bones and flesh of my flesh; she shall be called Woman, because she was taken out of Man." Therefore a man leaves his father and his mother and cleaves to his wife, and they become one flesh. And the man and his wife were both naked, and were not ashamed.

or this

[Adam and Eve rebel against God and are cast out of the Garden of Eden]

A Reading (Lesson) from the Book of Genesis
[3:1-15(16-22)]

Now the serpent was more subtle than any other wild creature that the Lord God had made. He said to the woman, "Did God say, 'You shall not eat of any tree of the garden'?" And the woman said to the serpent, "We may eat of the fruit of the trees of the garden; but God said,

'You shall not eat of the fruit of the tree which is in the midst of the garden, neither shall you touch it, lest you die.' " But the serpent said to the woman, "You will not die. For God knows that when you eat of it your eyes will be opened, and you will be like God, knowing good and evil." So when the woman saw that the tree was good for food, and that it was a delight to the eyes, and that the tree was to be desired to make one wise, she took of its fruit and ate; and she also gave some to her husband, and he ate. Then the eyes of both were opened, and they knew that they were naked; and they sewed fig leaves together and made themselves aprons. And they heard the sound of the Lord God walking in the garden in the cool of the day, and the man and his wife hid themselves from the presence of the Lord God among the trees of the garden. But the Lord God called to the man, and said to him, "Where are you?" And he said, "I heard the sound of thee in the garden, and I was afraid, because I was naked; and I hid myself." He said, "Who told you that you were naked? Have you eaten of the tree of which I commanded you not to eat?" The man said, "The woman whom thou gavest to be with me, she gave me fruit of the tree, and I ate." Then the Lord God said to the woman, "What is this that you have done?" The woman said, "The serpent beguiled me, and I ate." The Lord God said to the serpent, "Because you have done this, cursed are you above all cattle, and above all wild animals; upon your belly you shall go, and dust you shall eat all the days of your life. I will put enmity between you and the woman, and between your seed and her seed; he shall bruise your head, and you shall bruise his heel."

To the woman he said, "I will greatly multiply your pain in childbearing; in pain you shall bring forth children, yet your desire shall be for your husband, and he shall rule over you." And to Adam he said,

"Because you have listened to the voice of your wife, and have eaten of the tree of which I commanded you, 'You shall not eat of it,' cursed is the ground because of you; in toil you shall eat of it all the days of your life; thorns and thistles it shall bring forth to you; and you shall eat the plants of the field. In the sweat of your face you shall eat till you return to the ground, for out of it you were taken; you are dust, and to dust you shall return." The man called his wife's name Eve, because she was the mother of all living. And the Lord God made for Adam and for his wife garments of skins, and clothed them. Then the Lord God said, "Behold, the man has become like one of us, knowing good and evil; and now, lest he put forth his hand and take also of the tree of life, and eat, and live for ever" — therefore the Lord God sent him forth from the garden of Eden, to till the ground from which he was taken.

or this

[God comforts his people and calls on them to prepare for redemption]

A Reading (Lesson) from the Book of Isaiah [40:1-11]

Comfort, comfort my people, says your God. Speak tenderly to Jerusalem, and cry to her that her warfare is ended, that her iniquity is pardoned, that she has received from the Lord's hand double for all her sins. A voice cries: "In the wilderness prepare the way of the Lord, make straight in the desert a highway for our God. Every valley shall be lifted up, and every mountain and hill be made low; the uneven ground shall become level, and the rough places a plain. And the glory of the Lord shall be revealed, and all flesh shall see it together, for the mouth of the Lord has spoken." A voice says, "Cry!" And I said, "What shall I cry?" All flesh is grass, and all its beauty is like the flower of the field. The grass withers, the flower fades, when the breath of the Lord blows upon it; surely the people is grass. The grass withers, the flower fades; but the word of our God will stand for ever. Get you up to a high mountain, O Zion, herald of good tidings; lift up your voice with strength, O Jerusalem, herald of good tidings, lift it up, fear not; say to the cities of Judah, "Behold your God!" Behold, the Lord God comes with might, and his arm rules for him; behold, his reward is with him, and his recompense before him. He will feed his flock like a shepherd, he will gather the lambs in his arms, he will carry them in his bosom, and gently lead those that are with young.

or this

[A new covenant is promised which will be written in our hearts]

A Reading (Lesson) from the Book of Jeremiah [31:31-34]

Behold, the days are coming, says the Lord, when I will make a new covenant with the house of Israel and the house of Judah, not like the covenant which I made with their fathers when I took them by the hand to bring them out of the land of Egypt, my covenant which they broke, though I was their husband, says the Lord. But this is the covenant which I will make with the house of Israel after those days, says the Lord: I will put my law within them, and I will write it upon their hearts; and I will be their God, and they shall be my people. And no longer shall each man teach his neighbor and each his brother, saying, "Know the Lord," for they shall all know me, from the least of them to the greatest, says the Lord; for I will forgive their iniquity, and I will remember their sin no more.

or this

[God is called upon to act and to come among us]

A Reading (Lesson) from the Book of Isaiah [64:1-9a]

O that thou wouldst rend the heavens and come down, that the mountains might quake at thy presence — as when fire kindles brushwood and the fire causes water to boil — to make thy name known to thy adversaries, and that the nations might tremble at thy presence! When thou didst terrible things which we looked not for, thou camest down, the mountains quaked at thy presence. From of old no one has heard or perceived by the ear, no eye has seen a God besides thee, who works for those who wait for him. Thou meetest him that joyfully works righteousness, those that remember thee in thy ways. Behold, thou wast angry, and we sinned; in our sins we have been a long time, and shall we be saved? We have all become like one who is unclean, and all our righteous deeds are like a polluted garment. We all fade like a leaf, and our iniquities, like the wind, take us away. There is no one that calls upon thy name, that bestirs himself to take hold of thee; for thou hast hid thy face from us, and hast delivered us into the hand of our iniquities. Yet, O Lord, thou art our Father; we are the clay, and thou art our potter; we are all the work of thy hand. Be not exceedingly angry, O Lord, and remember not inquity for ever.

or this

[God reveals his glory to the prophet and calls him to be his messenger]

A Reading (Lesson) from the Book of Isaiah [6:1-11]

In the year that King Uzzi'ah died I saw the Lord sitting upon a throne, high and lifted up; and his train filled the temple. Above him stood the seraphim; each had six wings: with two he covered his face, and with two he covered his feet, and with two he flew. And one called to another and said: "Holy, holy, holy is the Lord of hosts; the whole earth is full of his glory." And the foundations of the thresholds shook at the voice of him who called, and the house was filled with smoke. And I said: "Woe is me! For I am a man of unclean lips, and I dwell in the midst of a people of unclean lips; for my eyes have seen the King, the Lord of hosts!" Then flew one of the seraphim to me, having in his hand a burning coal which he had taken with tongs from the altar. And he touched my mouth, and said: "Behold, this has touched your lips; your guilt is taken away, and your sin forgiven." And I heard the voice of the Lord saying, "Whom shall I send, and who will go for us?" Then I said, "Here am I! Send me." And he said, "Go, and say to this people: 'Hear and hear, but do not understand; see and see, but do not perceive.' Make the heart of this people fat, and their ears heavy, and shut their eyes; lest they see with their eyes, and hear with their ears, and understand with their hearts, and turn and be healed." Then I said, "How long, O Lord?" And he said: "Until cities lie waste without inhabitant, and houses without men, and the land is utterly desolate."

or the following

[The prophet proclaims that God will come and save us]

A Reading (Lesson) from the Book of Isaiah [35:1-10]

The wilderness and the dry land shall be glad, the desert shall rejoice and blossom; like the crocus it shall blossom abundantly, and rejoice with joy and singing. The glory of Lebanon shall be given to it, the majesty of Carmel and Sharon. They shall see the glory of the Lord, the majesty of our God. Strengthen the weak hands, and make firm the feeble knees. Say to those who are of a fearful heart, "Be strong, fear not! Behold, your God will come with vengeance, with the recompense of God. He will come and save you." Then the eyes of the blind shall be opened, and the ears of the deaf unstopped; then shall the lame man leap like a hart, and the tongue of the dumb sing for joy. For waters shall break forth in the wilderness, and streams in the desert; the burning sand shall become a pool, and the thirsty ground springs of water; the haunt of jackals shall become a swamp, the grass shall become reeds and rushes. And a highway shall be there, and it shall be called the Holy Way; the unclean shall not pass over it, and fools shall not err therein. No lion shall be there, nor shall any ravenous beast come upon it; they shall not be found there, but the redeemed shall walk there. And the ransomed of the Lord shall return, and come to Zion with singing; everlasting joy shall be upon their heads; they shall obtain joy and gladness, and sorrow and sighing shall flee away.

or this

[The scribe Baruch urges the people to look east because salvation is at hand]

A Reading (Lesson) from the Book of Baruch [4:36—5:9]

Look toward the east, O Jerusalem, and see the joy that is coming to you from God! Behold, your sons are coming, whom you sent away; they are coming, gathered from east and west, at the word of the Holy One, rejoicing in the glory of God. Take off the garment of your sorrow and affliction, O Jerusalem, and put on for ever the beauty of the glory from God. Put on the robe of the righteousness from God; put on your head the diadem of the glory of the Everlasting. For God will show your splendor everywhere under heaven. For your name will for ever be called by God, "Peace of righteousness and glory of godliness." Arise, O Jerusalem, stand upon the height and look toward the east, and see your children gathered from west and east, at the word of the Holy One, rejoicing that God has remembered them. For they went forth from you on foot, led away by their enemies; but God will bring them back to you, carried in glory, as on a royal throne. For God has ordered that every high mountain and the everlasting hills be made low and the valleys filled up, to make level ground, so that Israel may walk safely in the glory of God. The woods and every fragrant tree have shaded Israel at God's command. For God will lead Israel with joy, in the light of his glory, with the mercy and righteousness that come from him.

or the following

[God promises that a child shall be conceived who will be known as "God with us"]

A Reading (Lesson) from the Book of Isaiah [7:10-15]

The Lord spoke to Ahaz, "Ask a sign of the Lord your God; let it be deep as Sheol or high as heaven." But Ahaz said, "I will not ask, and I will not put the Lord to the test." And he said, "Hear then, O house of David! Is it too little for you to weary men, that you weary my God also? Therefore the Lord himself will give you a sign. Behold, a young woman shall conceive and bear a son, and shall call his name Iman'u-el. He shall eat curds and honey when he knows how to refuse the evil and choose the good."

or this

[The one who is to rule Israel will be born in the village of Bethlehem]

A Reading (Lesson) from the Book of Micah [5:2-4]

You, O Bethlehem Eph'ratha, who are little to be among the clans of Judah, from you shall come forth for me one who is to be ruler in Israel, whose origin is from of old, from ancient days. Therefore, he shall give them up until the time when she who is in travail has brought forth; then the rest of his brethren shall return to the people of Israel. And he shall stand and feed his flock in the strength of the Lord, in the majesty of the name of the Lord his God. And they shall dwell secure, for now he shall be great to the ends of the earth.

or this

[The Spirit of the Lord will rest upon the Holy One]

A Reading (Lesson) from the Book of Isaiah [11:1-9]

There shall come forth a shoot from the stump of Jesse, and a branch shall grow out of his roots. And the Spirit of the Lord shall rest upon him, the spirit of wisdom and understanding, the spirit of counsel and might, the spirit of knowledge and the fear of the Lord. And his delight shall be in the fear of the Lord. He shall not judge by what his eyes see, or decide by what his ears hear; but with righteousness he shall judge the poor, and decide with equity for the meek of the earth, and he shall smite the earth with the rod of his mouth, and with the breath of his lips he shall slay the wicked. Righteousness shall be the girdle of his loins. The wolf shall dwell with the lamb, and the leopard shall lie down with the kid, and the calf and the lion and the fatling together, and a little child shall lead them. The cow and the bear shall feed; their young shall lie down together; and the lion shall eat straw like the ox. The sucking child shall play over the hole of the asp, and the weaned child shall put his hand on the adder's den. They shall not hurt or destroy in all my holy mountain; for the earth shall be full of the knowledge of the Lord as the waters cover the sea.

or this

[The Lord will be among us; we are summoned to rejoice and sing]

A Reading (Lesson) from the Book of Zephaniah [3:14-18]

Sing aloud, O daughter of Zion; shout, O Israel! Rejoice and exult with all your heart, O daughter of Jerusalem! The Lord has taken away the judgments against you, he has cast out your enemies. The King of Israel, the Lord, is in your midst; you shall fear evil no more. On that day it shall be said to Jerusalem: "Do not fear, O Zion; let not your hands grow weak. The Lord, your God, is in your midst, a warrior who gives victory; he will rejoice over you with gladness, he will renew you in his love; he will exult over you with loud singing as on a day of festival.

or this

[God promises a new heaven and a new earth]

A Reading (Lesson) from the Book of Isaiah [65:17-25]

Thus says the Lord, "For behold, I create new heavens and a new earth; and the former things shall not be remembered or come into mind. But be glad and rejoice for ever in that which I create; for behold, I create Jerusalem a rejoicing, and her people a joy. I will rejoice in Jerusalem, and be glad in my people; no more shall be heard in it the sound of weeping and the cry of distress. No more shall there be in it an infant that lives but a few days, or an old man who does not fill out his days, for the child shall die a hundred years old, and the sinner a hundred years old shall be accursed. They shall build houses and inhabit them; they shall plant vineyards and eat their fruit. They shall not build and another inhabit; they shall not plant and another eat; for like the days of a tree shall the days of my people be, and my chosen shall long enjoy the work of their hands. They shall not labor in vain, or bear children for calamity; for they shall be the offspring of the blessed of the Lord, and their children with them. Before they call I will answer, while they are yet speaking I will hear. The wolf and the lamb shall feed together, the lion shall eat straw like the ox; and dust shall be the serpent's food. They shall not hurt or destroy in all my holy mountain, says the Lord."

If it is desired that the Lessons end with a reading from the Gospel, one of the following may be used:

[An angel announces to Zechari'ah that his wife Elizabeth will bear a son.]

✝ *The Holy Gospel of Our Lord Jesus Christ According to Luke* [1:5-25]

In the days of Herod, king of Judea, there was a priest named Zechari'ah, of the division of Abi'jah; and he had a wife of the daughters of Aaron, and her name was Elizabeth. And they were both righteous before God, walking in all the commandments and ordinances of the Lord blameless. But they had no child, because Elizabeth was barren, and both were advanced in years. Now while he was serving as priest before God when his division was on duty, according to the custom of the priesthood, it fell to him by lot to enter the temple of the Lord and burn incense. And the whole multitude of the people were praying outside at the hour of incense. And there appeared to him an angel of the Lord standing on the right side of the altar of incense. And Zechari'ah was troubled when he saw him, and fear fell upon him. But the angel said to him, "Do not be afraid, Zechari'ah, for your prayer is heard, and your wife Elizabeth will bear you a son, and you shall call his name John. And you will have joy and gladness, and many will rejoice at his birth; for he will be great before the Lord, and he shall drink no wine nor strong drink, and he will be filled with the Holy Spirit, even from his mother's womb. And he will turn many of the sons of Israel to the Lord their God, and he will go before him in the spirit and power of Eli'jah, to turn the hearts of the fathers to the children, and the disobedient to the wisdom of the just, to make ready for the Lord a people prepared." And Zechari'ah said to the angel, "How shall I know this? For I am an old man, and my wife is advanced in years." And the angel answered him, "I am Gabriel, who stand in the presence of God; and I was sent to speak to you, and to bring you this good news. And behold, you will be silent and unable to speak until the day that these things come to pass, because you did not believe my words, which will be fulfilled in their time." And the people were waiting for Zechari'ah, and they wondered at his delay in the temple. And when he came out, he could not speak to them, and they perceived that he had seen a vision in the temple; and he made signs to them and remained dumb. And when his time of service was ended, he went to his home. After these days his wife Elizabeth conceived, and for five months she hid herself, saying, "Thus the Lord has done to me in the days when he looked on me, to take away my reproach among men."

or this

[The Angel Gabriel announces to the Virgin Mary that she will bear the Son of the Most High]

✝ *The Holy Gospel of Our Lord Jesus Christ According to Luke* [1:26-38(39-56)]

In the sixth month the angel Gabriel was sent from God to a city of Galilee named Nazareth, to a virgin betrothed to a man whose name was Joseph, of the house of David; and the virgin's name was Mary. And he came to her and said, "Hail, O favored one, the Lord is with you!" But she was greatly troubled at the saying, and considered in her mind what sort of greeting this might be. And the angel said to her, "Do not be afraid, Mary, for you have found favor with God. And behold, you will conceive in your womb and bear a son, and you shall call his name Jesus. He will be great, and will be called the Son of the Most High; and the Lord God will give to him the throne of his father David, and he will reign over the house of Jacob for ever; and of his kingdom there will be no end." And Mary said to the angel, "How shall this be, since I have no husband?" And the angel said to her, "The Holy Spirit will come upon you, and the power of the Most High will overshadow you; therefore the child to be born will be called holy, the Son of God. And behold, your kinswoman Elizabeth in her old age has also conceived a son; and this is the sixth month with her who was called barren. For with God nothing will be impossible." And Mary said, "Behold, I am the handmaid of the Lord, let it be to me according to your word." And the angel departed from her.

In those days Mary arose and went with haste into the hill country, to a city of Judah, and she entered the house of Zechari'ah and greeted Elizabeth. And when Elizabeth heard the greeting of Mary, the babe leaped in her womb; and Elizabeth was filled with the Holy Spirit and she exclaimed with a loud cry, "Blessed are you among women, and blessed is the fruit of your womb! And why is this granted me, that the mother of my Lord should come to me? For behold, when the voice of your greeting came to my ears, the babe in my womb leaped for joy. And blessed is she who believed that there would be a fulfilment of what was spoken to her from the Lord." And Mary said, "My soul magnifies the Lord, and my spirit rejoices in God my Savior, for he has regarded the low estate of his handmaiden. For behold, henceforth all generations will call me blessed; for he who is mighty has done great things for me, and holy is his name. And his mercy is on those who fear him from generation to generation. He has shown strength with his arm, he has scattered the proud in the imagination of their hearts, he has put down the mighty from their thrones, and exalted those of low degree; he has filled the hungry with good things, and the rich he has sent empty away. He has helped his servant Israel, in remembrance of his mercy, as he spoke to our fathers, to Abraham and to his posterity for ever." And Mary remained with her about three months, and returned to her home.

Vigil for Christmas Eve or Christmas Festival of Lessons and Music

[BOS, page 38]

The Lessons

Nine Lessons are customarily selected (but fewer may be used), interspersed with appropriate carols, hymns, canticles, and anthems. When possible, each lesson is read by a different lector. The lesson from the third chapter of Genesis is never omitted.

The Lessons may be read without announcement or conclusion, or in the manner prescribed in the Daily Office.

FROM THE OLD TESTAMENT

[God creates man and woman to live in obedience to him in the Garden of Eden]

A Reading (Lesson) from the Book of Genesis [2:4b-9,15-25]

In the day that the Lord God made the earth and the heaven, when no plant of the field had yet sprung up—for the Lord God had not caused it to rain upon the earth, and there was no man to till the ground; but a mist went up from the earth and watered the whole face of the ground—then the Lord God formed man of dust from the ground, and breathed into his nostrils the breath of life; and man became a living being. And the Lord God planted a garden in Eden, in the east; and there he put the man whom he had formed. And out of the ground the Lord

God made to grow every tree that is pleasant to the sight and good for food, the tree of life also in the midst of the garden and the tree of the knowledge of good and evil. The Lord God took the man and put him in the garden of Eden to till it and keep it. And the Lord God commanded the man, saying, "You may freely eat of every tree of the garden; but of the tree of the knowledge of good and evil you shall not eat, for in the day that you eat of it you shall die." Then the Lord God said, "It is not good that the man should be alone; I will make him a helper fit for him." So out of the ground the Lord God formed every beast of the field and every bird of the air, and brought them to the man to see what he would call them; and whatever the man called every living creature, that was its name. The man gave names to all cattle, and to the birds of the air, and to every beast of the field; but for the man there was not found a helper fit for him. So the Lord God caused a deep sleep to fall upon the man, and while he slept took one of his ribs and closed up its place with flesh; and the rib which the Lord God had taken from the man he made into a woman and brought her to the man. Then the man said, "This at last is bone of my bones and flesh of my flesh; she shall be called Woman, because she was taken out of Man." Therefore a man leaves his father and his mother and cleaves to his wife, and they become one flesh. And the man and his wife were both naked, and were not ashamed.

[Adam and Eve rebel against God and are cast out of the Garden of Eden]

A Reading (Lesson) from the Book of Genesis
[3:1-15(16-23)]

Now the serpent was more subtle than any other wild creature that the Lord God had made. He said to the woman, "Did God say, 'You shall not eat of any tree of the garden'?" And the woman said to the serpent, "We may eat of the fruit of the trees of the garden; but God said, 'You shall not eat of the fruit of the tree which is in the midst of the garden, neither shall you touch it, lest you die.' " But the serpent said to the woman, "You will not die. For God knows that when you eat of it your eyes will be opened, and you will be like God, knowing good and evil." So when the woman saw that the tree was good for food, and that it was a delight to the eye, and that the tree was to be desired to make one wise, she took of its fruit and ate; and she also gave some to her husband, and he ate. Then the eyes of both were opened, and they knew that they were naked; and they sewed fig leaves together and made themselves aprons. And they heard the sound of the Lord God walking in the garden in the cool of the day, and the man and his wife hid themselves from the presence of the Lord God among the trees of the garden. But the Lord God called to the man, and said to him, "Where are you?" And he said, "I heard the sound of thee in the garden, and I was afraid, because I was naked; and I hid myself." He said, "Who told you that you were naked? Have you eaten of the tree of which I commanded you not to eat?" The man said, "The woman whom thou gavest to be with me, she gave me fruit of the tree, and I ate." Then the Lord God said to the woman, "What is this that you have done? The woman said, "The serpent beguiled me, and I ate." The Lord God said to the serpent, "Because you have done this, cursed are you above all cattle, and above all wild animals; upon your belly you shall go, and dust you shall eat all the days of your life. I will put enmity between you and the woman, and between your seed and her seed; he shall bruise your head, and you shall bruise his heel."

To the woman he said, "I will greatly multiply your pain in childbearing; in pain you shall bring forth children, yet your desire shall be for your husband, and he shall rule over you." And to Adam he said, "Because you have listened to the voice of your wife, and have eaten of the tree of which I commanded you, 'You shall not eat of it,' cursed is the ground because of you; in toil you shall eat of it all the days of your life; thorns and thistles it shall bring forth to you; and you shall eat the plants of the field. In the sweat of your face you shall eat bread till you return to the ground, for out of it you were taken; you are dust, and to dust you shall return." The man called his wife's name Eve, because she was the mother of all living. And the Lord God made for Adam and for his wife garments of skins, and clothed them. Then the Lord God said, "Behold, the man has become like one of us, knowing good and evil; and now, lest be put forth his hand and take also of the tree of life, and eat, and live for ever" — the Lord God sent him forth from the garden of Eden, to till the ground from which he was taken.

or this

[God comforts his people and calls on them to prepare for redemption]

A Reading (Lesson) from the Book of Isaiah [40:1-11]

Comfort, comfort my people, says your God. Speak tenderly to Jerusalem, and cry to her that her warfare is ended, that her iniquity is pardoned, that she has received from the Lord's hand double for all her sins. A voice cries: "In the wilderness prepare the way of the Lord, make straight in the desert a highway for our God. Every valley shall be lifted up, and every mountain and hill be made low; the uneven ground shall become level, and the rough places a plain. And the glory of the Lord shall be revealed, and all flesh shall see it together, for the mouth of the Lord has spoken." A voice says, "Cry!" And I said, "What shall I cry?" All flesh is grass, and all its beauty is like the flower of the field. The grass withers, the flower fades, when the breath of the Lord blows upon it; surely the people is grass. The grass withers, the flower fades; but the word of our God will stand for ever. Get you up to a high mountain, O Zion, herald of good tidings; lift up your voice with strength, O Jerusalem, herald of good tidings, lift it up, fear not; say to the cities of Judah, "Behold your God!" Behold, the Lord God comes with might, and his arm rules for him; behold, his reward is with him, and his recompense before him. He will feed his flock like a shepherd, he will gather the lambs in his arms, he will carry them in his bosom, and gently lead those that are with young.

or the following

[The prophet proclaims that God will come and save us]

A Reading (Lesson) from the Book of Isaiah [35:1-10]

The wilderness and the dry land shall be glad, the desert shall rejoice and blossom; like the crocus it shall blossom abundantly, and rejoice with joy and singing. The glory of Lebanon shall be given to it, the majesty of Carmel and Sharon. They shall see the glory of the Lord, the majesty of our God. Strengthen the weak hands, and make firm the feeble knees. Say to those who are of a fearful heart, "Be strong, fear not! Behold, your God will come with vengeance, with the recompense of God. He will come and save you." Then the eyes of the blind shall be opened, and the ears of the deaf unstopped; then shall the lame man leap like a hart, and the tongue of the dumb sing for joy. For waters shall break forth in the wilderness, and streams in the desert; the burning sand shall become a pool, and the thirsty ground springs of water; the haunt of jackals shall become a swamp, the grass shall become reeds and rushes. And a highway shall be there, and it shall be called the Holy Way; the unclean shall not pass over it, and fools shall not err therein. No lion shall be there, nor shall any ravenous beast come upon it; they shall not be found there, but the redeemed shall walk there. And the ransomed of the Lord shall return, and come to Zion with singing; everlasting joy shall be upon their heads; they shall obtain joy and gladness, and sorrow and sighing shall flee away.

or this

[God promises that a child shall be conceived who will be known as "God with us"]

A Reading (Lesson) from the Book of Isaiah [7:10-15]

The Lord spoke to Ahaz, "Ask a sign of the Lord your God; let it be deep as Sheol or high as heaven." But Ahaz said, "I will not ask, and I will not put the Lord to the test." And he said, "Hear then, O house of David! Is it too little for you to weary men, that you weary my God also? Therefore the Lord himself will give you a sign. Behold, a young woman shall conceive and bear a son, and shall call his name Iman'u-el. He shall eat curds and honey when he knows how to refuse the evil and choose the good."

FROM THE NEW TESTAMENT

[An angel announces to Zechari'ah that his wife Elizabeth will bear a son]

A Reading (Lesson) from the Gospel According to Luke [1:5-25] [page 99 above]

or this

[The Angel Gabriel announces to the Virgin Mary that she will bear the Son of the Most High]

A Reading (Lesson) from the Gospel According to Luke [1:26-58]

In the sixth month the angel Gabriel was sent from God to a city of Galilee named Nazareth, to a virgin betrothed to a man whose name was Joseph, of the house of David; and the virgin's name was Mary. And he came to her and said,

"Hail, O favored one, the Lord is with you!" But she was greatly troubled at the saying, and considered in her mind what sort of greeting this might be. And the angel said to her, "Do not be afraid, Mary, for you have found favor with God. And behold, you will conceive in your womb and bear a son, and you shall call his name Jesus. He will be great, and will be called the Son of the Most High; and the Lord God will give to him the throne of his father David, and he will reign over the house of Jacob for ever; and of his kingdom there will be no end." And the angel said to her, "The Holy Spirit will come upon you, and the power of the Most High will overshadow you; therefore the child to be born will be called holy, the Son of God. And behold, your kinswoman Elizabeth in her old age has also conceived a son; and this is the sixth month with her who was called barren. For with God nothing will be impossible." And Mary said, "Behold, I am the handmaid of the Lord; let it be to me according to your word." And the angel departed from her. In those days Mary arose and went with haste into the hill country, to a city of Judah, and she entered the house of Zechari'ah and greeted Elizabeth. And when Elizabeth heard the greeting of Mary, the babe leaped in her womb; and Elizabeth was filled with the Holy Spirit and she exclaimed with a loud cry, "Blessed are you among women, and blessed is the fruit of your womb! And why is this granted me, that the mother of my Lord should come to me? For behold, when the voice of your greeting came to my ears, the babe in my womb leaped for joy. And blessed is she who believed that there would be a fulfilment of what was spoken to her from the Lord." And Mary said, "My soul magnifies the Lord, and my spirit rejoices in God my Savior, for he has regarded the low estate of his handmaiden. For behold, henceforth all generations will call me blessed; for he who is mighty has done great things for me, and holy is his name. And his mercy is on those who fear him from generation to generation. He has shown strength with his arm, he has scattered the proud in the imagination of their hearts, he has put down the mighty from their thrones, and exalted those of low degree; he has filled the hungry with good things, and the rich he has sent empty away. He has helped his servant Israel, in remembrance of his mercy, as he spoke to our fathers, to Abraham and to his posterity for ever." And Mary remained with her about three months, and returned to her home. Now the time came for Elizabeth to be delivered, and she gave birth to a son. And her neighbors and kinsfolk heard that the Lord had shown great mercy to her, and they rejoiced with her.

or this

[The Virgin Mary is greeted by Elizabeth and proclaims her joy]

A Reading (Lesson) from the Gospel According to Luke [1:39-46(47-56)]

In those days Mary arose and went with haste into the hill country, to a city of Judah, and she entered the house of Zechari'ah and greeted Elizabeth. And when Elizabeth heard the greeting of Mary, the babe leaped in her womb; and Elizabeth was filled with the Holy Spirit and she exclaimed with a loud cry, "Blessed are you among women, and blessed is the fruit of your womb! And why is this granted me, that the mother of my Lord should come to me? For behold, when the voice of your greeting came to my ears, the babe in my womb leaped for joy. And blessed is she who believed that there would be a fulfilment of what was spoken to her from the Lord." And Mary said, "My soul magnifies the Lord."

"and my spirit rejoices in God my Savior, for he has
regarded the low estate of his handmaiden. For behold,
henceforth all generations will call me blessed; for he
who is mighty has done great things for me, and holy is
his name. And his mercy is on those who fear him from
generation to generation. He has shown strength with
his arm, he has scattered the proud in the imagination
of their hearts, he has put down the mighty from their
thrones, and exalted those of low degree; he has filled
the hungry with good things, and the rich he has sent
empty away. He has helped his servant Israel, in
remembrance of his mercy, as he spoke to our fathers,
to Abraham and to his posterity for ever." And Mary
remained with her about three months, and returned to
her home.

or this

**[John the Baptist is born and his father rejoices that his
son will prepare the way of the Lord]**

A Reading (Lesson) from the Gospel According to Luke
[1:57-80]

The time came for Elizabeth to be delivered, and she gave
birth to a son. And her neighbors and kinsfolk heard that
the Lord had shown great mercy to her, and they rejoiced
with her. And on the eighth day they came to circumcise
the child; and they would have named him Zechari'ah
after his father, but his mother said, "Not so; he shall be
called John." And they said to her, "None of your kindred
is called by this name." And they made signs to his father,
inquiring what he would have him called. And he asked
for a writing tablet, and wrote, "His name is John." And
they all marveled. And immediately his mouth was opened

and his tongue loosed, and he spoke, blessing God. And fear came on all their neighbors. And all these things were talked about through all the hill country of Judea; and all who heard them laid them up in their hearts, saying, "What then will this child be?" For the hand of the Lord was with him. And his father Zechari'ah was filled with the Holy Spirit, and prophesied, saying, "Blessed be the Lord God of Israel, for he has visited and redeemed his people, and has raised up a horn of salvation for us in the house of his servant David, as he spoke by the mouth of his holy prophets from of old, that we should be saved from our enemies, and from the hand of all who hate us; to perform the mercy promised to our fathers, and to remember his holy covenant, the oath which he swore to our father Abraham, to grant that we, being delivered from the hand of our enemies, might serve him without fear, in holiness and righteousness before him all the days of our life. And you, child, will be called the prophet of the Most High; for you will go before the Lord to prepare his ways, to give knowledge of salvation to his people in the forgiveness of their sins, through the tender mercy of our God, when the day shall dawn upon us from on high to give light to those who sit in darkness and in the shadow of death, to guide our feet into the way of peace." And the child grew and became strong in spirit, and he was in the wilderness till the day of his manifestation to Israel.

or the following

[Jesus is born at Bethlehem and is worshiped by angels and shepherds]

A Reading (Lesson) from the Gospel According to Luke
[2:1-20]

In those days a decree went out from Caesar Augustus that all the world should be enrolled. This was the first enrollment, when Quirin'i-us was governor of Syria. And all went to be enrolled, each to his own city. And Joseph also went up from Galilee, from the city of Nazareth, to Judea, to the city of David, which is called Bethlehem, because he was of the house and lineage of David, to be enrolled with Mary, his betrothed, who was with child. And while they were there, the time came for her to be delivered. And she gave birth to her first-born son and wrapped him in swaddling cloths, and laid him in a manger, because there was no place for them in the inn. And in that region there were shepherds out in the field, keeping watch over their flock by night. And an angel of the Lord appeared to them, and the glory of the Lord shone around them, and they were filled with fear. And the angel said to them, "Be not afraid; for behold, I bring you good news of a great joy which will come to all the people; for to you is born this day in the city of David a Savior, who is Christ the Lord. And this will be a sign for you: you will find a babe wrapped in swaddling cloths and lying in a manger." And suddenly there was with the angel a multitude of the heavenly host praising God and saying, "Glory to God in the highest, and on earth peace among men with whom he is pleased!" When the angels went away from them into heaven, the shepherds said to one another, "Let us go over to Bethlehem and see this thing that has happened, which the Lord has made known to us." And they went with haste, and found Mary and Joseph, and the babe lying in a manger. And when they saw it they made known the saying which had been told them concerning this child; and all who heard it wondered at what the shepherds told them. But Mary kept all these things, pondering them in her heart. And the shepherds returned, glorifying and praising God for all they had heard and seen, as it had been told them.

or this

[Jesus receives his name and is presented to Simeon in the Temple]

A Reading (Lesson) from the Gospel According to Luke [2:21-36]

At the end of eight days, when he was circumcised, he was called Jesus, the name given by the angel before he was conceived in the womb. And when the time came for their purification according to the law of Moses, they brought him up to Jerusalem to present him to the Lord (as it is written in the law of the Lord, "Every male that opens the womb shall be called holy to the Lord") and to offer a sacrifice according to what is said in the law of the Lord, "a pair of turtledoves, or two young pigeons." Now there was a man in Jerusalem, whose name was Simeon, and this man was righteous and devout, looking for the consolation of Israel, and the Holy Spirit was upon him. And it had been revealed to him by the Holy Spirit that he should not see death before he had seen the Lord's Christ. And inspired by the Spirit he came into the temple; and when the parents brought in the child Jesus, to do for him according to the custom of the law, he took him up in his arms and blessed God and said, "Lord, now lettest thou thy servant depart in peace, according to thy word; for mine eyes have seen thy salvation which thou hast prepared in the presence of all people, a light for revelation to the Gentiles, and for glory to thy people Israel." And his father and his mother marveled at what was said about him; and Simeon blessed them and said to Mary his mother, "Behold, this child is set for the fall and rising of many in Israel, and for a sign that is spoken against (and a sword will pierce through your own soul also), that thoughts out of many hearts may be revealed." And there was a prophetess, Anna, the daughter of Phan'u-el, of the tribe of Asher; she was of a great age, having lived with her husband seven years from her virginity.

or this

[In the fullness of time, God sent his Son whose reign is for ever and ever]

A Reading (Lesson) from the Letter to the Hebrews
[1:1-12]

In many and various ways God spoke of old to our fathers by the prophets; but in these last days he has spoken to us by a Son, whom he appointed the heir of all things, through whom also he created the world. He reflects the glory of God and bears the very stamp of his nature, upholding the universe by his word of power. When he had made purification for sins, he sat down at the right hand of the Majesty on high, having become as much superior to angels as the name he has obtained is more excellent than theirs. For to what angel did God ever say, "Thou art my Son, today I have begotten thee"? Or again, "I will be to him a father, and he shall be to me a son"? And again, when he brings the first-born into the world, he says, "Let all God's angels worship him." Of the angels he says, "Who makes his angels winds, and his servants flames of fire." But of the Son he says, "Thy throne, O God, is for ever and ever, the righteous scepter is the scepter of thy kingdom. Thou has loved righteousness and hated lawlessness; therefore God, thy God, has anointed thee with the oil of gladness beyond thy comrades." And, "Thou, Lord, didst found the earth in the beginning, and the heavens are the work of thy hands; they will perish, but thou remainest; they will all grow old like a garment, like a mantle thou wilt roll them up, and they will be changed. But thou art the same, and thy years will never end."

or this

[The Word was made flesh and we have seen his glory]

A Reading (Lesson) from the Gospel According to John [1:1-18]

In the beginning was the Word, and the Word was with God, and the Word was God. He was in the beginning with God; all things were made through him, and without him was not anything made that was made. In him was life, and the life was the light of men. The light shines in the darkness, and the darkness has not overcome it. There was a man sent from God, whose name was John. He came for testimony, to bear witness to the light, that all might believe through him. He was not the light, but came to bear witness to the light. The true light that enlightens every man was coming into the world. He was in the world, and the world was made through him, yet the world knew him not. He came to his own home, and his own people received him not. But to all who received him, who believed in his name, he gave power to become children of God; who were born, not of blood nor of the will of the flesh nor of the will of man, but of God. And the Word became flesh and dwelt among us, full of grace and truth; we have beheld his glory, glory as of the only Son from the Father. (John bore witness to him, and cried, "This was he of whom I said, 'He who comes after me ranks before me, for he was before me.' ") And from his fulness have we all received, grace upon grace. For the law was given through Moses; grace and truth came through Jesus Christ. No one has ever seen God; the only Son, who is in the bosom of the Father, he has made him known.

Service for New Year's Eve
[BOS, page 40]

FROM THE OLD TESTAMENT

[The Hebrew Year]

A Reading (Lesson) from the Book of Exodus
[23:9-16, 20-21]

The Lord said to Moses, "Thus you shall say to the people of Israel: you shall not oppress a stranger; you know the heart of a stranger, for you were strangers in the land of Egypt. For six years you shall sow your land and gather in its yield; but the seventh year you shall let it rest and lie fallow, that the poor of your people may eat; and what they leave the wild beasts may eat. You shall do likewise with your vineyard, and with your olive orchard. Six days you shall do your work, but on the seventh day you shall rest; that your ox and your ass may rest, and the son of your bondmaid, and the alien, may be refreshed. Take heed to all that I have said to you; and make no mention of the names of other gods, nor let such be heard out of your mouth. Three times in the year you shall keep a feast to me. You shall keep the feast of unleavened bread; as I commanded you, you shall eat unleavened bread for seven days at the appointed time in the month of Abib, for in it you came out of Egypt. None shall appear before me empty-handed. You shall keep the feast of harvest, of the first fruits of your labor, of what you sow in the field. You shall keep the feast of ingathering at the end of the year, when you gather in from the field the fruit of your labor."

Psalm 111 [page 754] or *Psalm 119:1-8* [page 763]

[The promised land]

A Reading (Lesson) from the Book of Deuteronomy [11:8-12,26-28]

Moses said to the people, "You shall keep all the commandments which I command you this day, that you may be strong, and go in and take possession of the land which you are going over to possess, and that you may live long in the land which the Lord swore to your fathers to give to them and to their descendants, a land flowing with milk and honey. For the land which you are entering to take possession of it is not like the land of Egypt, from which you have come, where you sowed your seed and watered it with your feet, like a garden of vegetables; but the land which you are going over to possess is a land of hills and valleys, which drinks water by the rain from heaven."

Psalm 36:5-10 [page 632] or *Psalm 89, Part I* [page 713]

[A season for all things]

A Reading (Lesson) from the Book of Ecclesiastes
[3:1-15]

For everything there is a season, and a time for every matter under heaven: a time to be born, and a time to die; a time to plant, and a time to pluck up what is planted; a time to kill, and a time to heal; a time to break down, and a time to build up; a time to weep, and a time to laugh; a time to mourn, and a time to dance; a time to cast away stones, and a time to gather stones together; a time to embrace, and a time to refrain from embracing; a time to seek, and a time to lose; a time to keep, and a time to cast away; a time to rend, and a time to sew; a time to keep silence, and a time to speak; a time to love, and a time to hate; a time for war, and a time for peace. What gain has the worker from his toil? I have seen the business that God has given to the sons of men to be busy with. He has made everything beautiful in its time; also he has put eternity into man's mind, yet so that he cannot find out what God has done from the beginning to the end. I know that there is nothing better for them than to be happy and enjoy themselves as long as they live; also that it is God's gift to man that every one should eat and drink and take pleasure in all his toil. I know that whatever God does endures for ever; nothing can be added to it, nor anything taken from it; God has made it so, in order that men should fear before him. That which is, already has been; that which is to be, already has been; and God seeks what has been driven away.

Psalm 90 [page 717]

[Remember your Creator]

A Reading (Lesson) from the Book of Ecclesiastes
[12:1-8]

Remember your Creator in the days of your youth, before
the evil days come, and the years draw nigh, when you
will say, "I have no pleasure in this"; before the sun and
the light and the moon and the stars are darkened and the
clouds return after the rain; in the day when the keepers of
the house tremble, and the strong men are bent, and the
grinders cease because they are few, and those that look
through the windows are dimmed, and the doors on the
street are shut; when the sound of the grinding is low, and
one rises up at the voice of a bird, and all the daughters of
song are brought low; they are afraid also of what is high,
and terrors are in the way; the almond tree blossoms, the
grasshopper drags itself along and desire fails; because
man goes to his eternal home, and the mourners go about
the streets; before the silver cord is snapped, or the golden
bowl is broken, or the pitcher is broken at the fountain, or
the wheel broken at the cistern, and the dust returns to the
earth as it was, and the spirit returns to God who gave it.
Vanity of vanities, says the Preacher; all is vanity.

Psalm 130 [page 784]

[Marking the times, and winter]

A Reading (Lesson) from the Book of Ecclesiasticus
[43:1-22]

The pride of the heavenly heights is the clear firmament,
the appearance of heaven in a spectacle of glory. The sun,
when it appears, making proclamation as it goes forth, is a
marvelous instrument, the work of the Most High. At

noon it parches the land; and who can withstand its burning heat? A man tending a furnace works in burning heat, but the sun burns the mountains three times as much; it breathes out fiery vapors, and with bright beams it blinds the eyes. Great is the Lord who made it; and at his command it hastens on its course. He made the moon also, to serve in its season to mark the times and to be an everlasting sign. From the moon comes the sign for feast days, a light that wanes when it has reached the full. The month is named for the moon, increasing marvelously in its phases, an instrument of the hosts on high shining forth in the firmament of heaven. The glory of the stars is the beauty of heaven, a gleaming array in the heights of the Lord. At the command of the Holy One they stand as ordered, they never relax in their watches. Look upon the rainbow, and praise him who made it, exceedingly beautiful in its brightness. It encircles the heaven with its glorious arc; the hands of the Most High have stretched it out. By his command he sends the driving snow and speeds the lightnings of his judgment. Therefore the storehouses are opened, and the clouds fly forth like birds. In his majesty he amasses the clouds, and the hailstones are broken in pieces. At his appearing the mountains are shaken; at his will the south wind blows. The voice of his thunder rebukes the earth; so do the tempest from the north and the whirlwind. He scatters the snow like birds flying down, and its descent is like locusts alighting. The eye marvels at the beauty of its whiteness, and the mind is amazed at its falling. He pours the hoarfrost upon the earth like salt, and when it freezes, it becomes pointed thorns. The cold north wind blows, and ice freezes over the water; it rests upon every pool of water, and the water puts it on like a breastplate. He consumes the mountains and burns up the wilderness, and withers the tender grass like fire. A mist quickly heals all things; when the dew appears, it refreshes from the heat.

Psalm 19 [page 606] or *Psalm 148* [page 805] or
Psalm 74:11-22 [page 690]

FROM THE NEW TESTAMENT

[The acceptable time]

A Reading (Lesson) from the Second Letter of Paul to the Corinthians [5:17—6:2]

If any one is in Christ, he is a new creation; the old has passed away, behold, the new has come. All this is from God, who through Christ reconciled us to himself and gave us the ministry of reconciliation; that is, in Christ God was reconciling the world to himself, not counting their trespasses against them, and entrusting to us the message of reconciliation. So we are ambassadors for Christ, God making his appeal through us. We beseech you on behalf of Christ, be reconciled to God. For our sake he made him to be sin who knew no sin, so that in him we might become the righteousness of God. Working together with him, then, we entreat you not to accept the grace of God in vain. For he says, "At the acceptable time I have listened to you, and helped you on the day of salvation." Behold, now is the acceptable time; behold, now is the day of salvation.

Psalm 63:1-8 [page 670] or
Canticle 5 or 17 [page 51 or 93]

[While it is called today]

A Reading (Lesson) from the Letter to the Hebrews
[3:1-15(16—4:13)]

Now my holy brethren, who share in a heavenly call, consider Jesus, the apostle and high priest of our confession. He was faithful to him who appointed him, just as Moses also was faithful in God's house. Yet Jesus has been counted worthy of as much more glory than Moses as the builder of a house has more honor than the house. (For every house is built by some one, but the builder of all things is God.) Now Moses was faithful in all God's house as a servant, to testify to the things that were to be spoken later, but Christ was faithful over God's house as a son. And we are his house if we hold fast our confidence and pride in our hope. Therefore, as the Holy Spirit says, "Today, when you hear his voice, do not harden your hearts as in the rebellion, on the day of testing in the wilderness, where your fathers put me to the test and saw my works for forty years. Therefore I was provoked with that generation, and said, 'They always go astray in their hearts; they have not known my ways,' And I swore in my wrath, 'They shall never enter my rest.' " Take care, brethren, lest there be in any of you an evil, unbelieving heart, leading you to fall away from the living God. But exhort one another every day, as long as it is called "today," that none of you may be hardened by the deceitfulness of sin. For we share in Christ, if only we hold our first confidence firm to the end, while it is said, "Today, when you hear his voice, do not harden your hearts as in the rebellion."

Who were they that heard and yet were rebellious? Was it not all those who left Egypt under the leadership of Moses? And with whom was he provoked forty years?

Was it not with those who sinned, whose bodies fell in the wilderness? And to whom did he swear that they should never enter his rest, but to those who were disobedient? So we see that they were unable to enter because of unbelief. Therefore, while the promise of entering his rest remains, let us fear lest any of you be judged to have failed to reach it. For good news came to us just as to them; but the message which they heard did not benefit them, because it did not meet with faith in the hearers. For we who have believed enter that rest, as he has said, "As I swore in my wrath, 'They shall never enter my rest,' " although his works were finished from the foundation of the world.

Psalm 95 [page 724]

[New heavens and new earth]

A Reading (Lesson) from the Revelation to John
[21:1-14,22-24]

I saw a new heaven and a new earth; for the first heaven and the first earth had passed away, and the sea was no more. And I saw the holy city, new Jerusalem, coming down out of heaven from God, prepared as a bride adorned for her husband; and I heard a loud voice from the throne saying, "Behold, the dwelling of God is with men. He will dwell with them, and they shall be his people, and God himself will be with them; he will wipe away every tear from their eyes, and death shall be no more, neither shall there be mourning nor crying nor pain any more, for the former things have passed away." And he who sat upon the throne said, "Behold, I make all things new." Also he said, "Write this, for these words are trustworthy and true." And he said to me, "It is done! I am the Alpha and the Omega, the beginning and the end.

To the thirsty I will give from the fountain of the water of life without payment. He who conquers shall have this heritage, and I will be his God and he shall be my son. But as for the cowardly, the faithless, the polluted, as for murderers, fornicators, sorcerers, idolaters, and all liars, their lot shall be in the lake that burns with fire and sulphur, which is the second death." Then came one of the seven angels who had the seven bowls full of the seven last plagues, and spoke to me, saying, "Come, I will show you the Bride, the wife of the Lamb": And in the Spirit he carried me away to a great, high mountain, and showed me the holy city Jerusalem coming down out of heaven from God, having the glory of God, its radiance like a most rare jewel, like a jasper, clear as crystal. It had a great, high wall, with twelve gates, and at the gates twelve angels, and on the gates the names of the twelve tribes of the sons of Israel were inscribed; on the east three gates, on the north three gates, on the south three gates, and on the west three gates. And the wall of the city had twelve foundations, and on them the twelve names of the twelve apostles of the Lamb. And I saw no temple in the city, for its temple is the Lord God the Almighty and the Lamb. And the city has no need of sun or moon to shine upon it, for the glory of God is its light, and its lamp is the Lamb. By its light shall the nations walk; and the kings of the earth shall bring their glory into it.

Canticle 19 [page 94]

Vigil for the Eve of the Baptism of Our Lord

[BOS, page 49]

FROM THE OLD TESTAMENT

[The story of the flood]

A Reading (Lesson) from the Book of Genesis
[(7:1-5,11-18);8:6-18;9:8-13]

The Lord said to Noah, "Go into the ark, you and all your household, for I have seen that you are righteous before me in this generation. Take with you seven pairs of all clean animals, the male and his mate; and a pair of the animals that are not clean, the male and his mate; and seven pairs of the birds of the air also, male and female, to keep their kind alive upon the face of all the earth. For in seven days I will send rain upon the earth forty days and forty nights; and every living thing that I have made I will blot out from the face of the ground." And Noah did all that the Lord had commanded him. In the six hundredth year of Noah's life, in the second month, on the seventeenth day of the month, on that day all the fountains of the great deep burst forth, and the windows of the heavens were opened. And rain fell upon the earth forty days and forty nights. On the very same day Noah and his sons, Shem and Ham and Japheth, and Noah's wife and the three wives of his sons with them entered the ark, they and every beast according to its kind, and all the cattle according to their kinds, and every creeping thing that creeps on the earth according to its kind, and every bird according to its kind, every bird of every sort. They went into the ark with Noah, two and two of all flesh in which there was the breath of life. And they that entered, male and female of all flesh, went in as God had commanded him; and the Lord shut him in. The flood continued forty days upon the earth; and the waters increased, and bore up the ark, and it rose high above the earth. The waters prevailed and increased greatly upon the earth; and the ark floated on the face of the waters.

At the end of forty days Noah opened the window of the ark which he had made, and sent forth a raven; and it went to and fro until the waters were dried up from the earth. Then he sent forth a dove from him, to see if the waters had subsided from the face of the ground; but the dove found no place to set her foot, and she returned to him to the ark, for the waters were still on the face of the whole earth. So he put forth his hand and took her and brought her into the ark with him. He waited another seven days, and again he sent forth the dove out of the ark; and the dove came back to him in the evening, and lo, in her mouth a freshly plucked olive leaf; so Noah knew that the waters had subsided from the earth. Then he waited another seven days, and sent forth the dove; and she did not return to him any more. In the six hundred and first year, in the first month, the first day of the month, the waters were dried from off the earth; and Noah removed the covering of the ark, and looked, and behold, the face of the ground was dry. In the second month, on the twenty-seventh day of the month, the earth was dry. Then God said to Noah, "Go forth from the ark, you and your wife, and your sons and your sons' wives with you. Bring forth with you every living thing that is with you of all flesh — birds and animals and every creeping thing that creeps on the earth — that they may breed abundantly on the earth, and be fruitful and multiply upon the earth." Then God said to Noah and to his sons with him, "Behold, I establish my covenant with you and your descendants after you, and with every living creature that is with you, the birds, the cattle, and every beast of the earth with you, as many as came out of the ark. I establish my covenant with you, that never again shall all flesh be cut off by the waters of a flood, and never again shall there be a flood to destroy the earth." And God said, "This is the sign of the covenant which I make between me and you and every living creature that is with you, for all future generations: I set my bow in the cloud, and it shall be a sign of the covenant between me and the earth."

Psalm 25:3-9 [page 614]   or   *Psalm 46* [page 649]

or this

[The Lord who makes a way in the sea]

A Reading (Lesson) from the Book of Isaiah [43:15-19]

Thus says the Lord, the Holy One of Israel: "I am the Lord, your Holy one, the Creator of Israel, your King." Thus says the Lord, who makes a way in the sea, a path in the mighty waters, who brings forth chariot and horse, army and warrior; they lie down, they cannot rise, they are extinguished, quenched like a wick: "Remember not the former things, nor consider the things of old. Behold, I am doing a new thing; now it springs forth, do you not perceive it? I will make a way in the wilderness and rivers in the desert."

Psalm 114 [page 756]

or the following

[The washing and anointing of Aaron]

A Reading (Lesson) from the Book of Leviticus [8:1-12]

The Lord said to Moses, "Take Aaron and his sons with him, and the garments, and the anointing oil, and the bull of the sin offering, and two rams, and the basket of unleavened bread; and assemble all the congregation at the door of the tent of meeting." And Moses did as the Lord commanded him; and the congregation was assembled at the door of the tent of meeting. And Moses said to the congregation, "This is the thing which the Lord has commanded to be done" And Moses brought Aaron and his sons, and washed them with water. And he put on him the coat, and girded him with the girdle, and clothed him with the robe, and put the ephod upon him, and girded him with the skilfully woven band of the ephod, binding it to him therewith. And he placed the breastpiece on him, and in the breastpiece he put the Urim and the Thummim. And he set the turban upon his head, and on the turban, in front, he set the golden plate, the holy crown, as the Lord commanded Moses. Then Moses took the anointing oil, and anointed the tabernacle and all that was in it, and consecrated them. And he sprinkled some of it on the altar seven times, and anointed the altar and all its utensils, and the laver and its base, to consecrate them. And he poured some of the anointing oil on Aaron's head, and anointed him, to consecrate him.

Psalm 23 [page 612]   or   *Psalm 133* [page 787]

or this

[The anointing of David]

A Reading (Lesson) from the First Book of Samuel
[16:1-13]

The Lord said to Samuel, "How long will you grieve over Saul, seeing I have rejected him from being king over Israel? Fill your horn with oil, and go; I will send you to Jesse the Bethlehemite, for I have provided for myself a king among his sons." And Samuel said, "How can I go? If Saul hears it, he will kill me." And the Lord said, "Take a heifer with you, and say, 'I have come to sacrifice to the Lord.' And invite Jesse to the sacrifice, and I will show you what you shall do; and you shall anoint for me him whom I name to you." Samuel did what the Lord commanded, and came to Bethlehem. The elders of the city came to meet him trembling, and said, "Do you come peaceably?" And he said, "Peaceably; I have come to sacrifice to the Lord; consecrate yourselves, and come with me to the sacrifice." And he consecrated Jesse and his sons, and invited them to the sacrifice. When they came, he looked on Eli'ab and thought, "Surely the Lord's anointed is before him." But the Lord said to Samuel, "Do not look on his appearance or on the height of his stature, because I have rejected him; for the Lord looks on the heart." Then Jesse called Abin'adab, and made him pass before Samuel. And he said, "Neither has the Lord chosen this one." Then Jesse made Shammah pass by. And he said, "Neither has the Lord chosen this one." And Jesse made seven of his sons pass before Samuel. And Samuel said to Jesse, "The Lord has not chosen these." And Samuel said to Jesse, "Are all your sons here?" And he said, "There remains yet the youngest, but behold, he is keeping the sheep." And Samuel said to Jesse, "Send and fetch him; for we will not sit down till be comes here." And he sent, and brought him in. Now he was ruddy, and had beautiful eyes, and was handsome. And the Lord said, "Arise, anoint him; for this is he." Then Samuel took the horn of oil, and anointed him in the midst of his brothers; and the Spirit of the Lord came mightily upon David from that day forward. And Samuel rose up, and went to Ramah.

Psalm 2:1-8 [page 586] or *Psalm 110:1-5* [page 753]

or this

[The cleansing of Na'aman in the Jordan]

A Reading (Lesson) from the Second Book of the Kings [5:1-14]

Na'aman, commander of the army of the king of Syria, was a great man with his master and in high favor, because by him the Lord had given victory to Syria. He was a mighty man of valor, but he was a leper. Now the Syrians on one of their raids had carried off a little maid from the land of Israel, and she waited on Na'aman's wife. She said to her mistress, "Would that my lord were with the prophet who is in Samar'ia! He would cure him of his leprosy." So Na'aman went in and told his lord, "Thus and so spoke the maiden from the land of Israel." And the king of Syria said, "Go now, and I will send a letter to the king of Israel." So he went, taking with him ten talents of silver, six thousand shekels of gold, and ten festal garments. And he brought the letter to the king of Israel, which read, "When this letter reaches you, know that I have sent to you Na'aman, my servant, that you may cure him of his leprosy." And when the king of Israel read the letter, he rent his clothes and said, "Am I God, to kill and to make alive, that this man sends word to me to cure a man of his leprosy? Only consider, and see how he is seeking a quarrel with me." But when Eli'sha the man of

God heard that the king of Israel had rent his clothes, he sent to the king, saying, "Why have you rent your clothes? Let him come now to me, that he may know that there is a prophet in Israel." So Na'aman came with his horses and chariots, and halted at the door of Eli'sha's house. And Eli'sha sent a messenger to him, saying, "Go and wash in the Jordan seven times, and your flesh shall be restored, and you shall be clean." But Na'aman was angry, and went away, saying, "Behold, I thought that he would surely come out to me, and stand, and call on the name of the Lord his God, and wave his hand over the place, and cure the leper. Are not Aba'na and Pharpar, the rivers of Damascus, better than all the waters of Israel? Could I not wash in them, and be clean?" So he turned and went away in a rage. But his servants came near and said to him, "My father, if the prophet had commanded you to do some great thing, would you not have done it? How much rather, then, when he says to you, 'Wash, and be clean'?" So he went down and dipped himself seven times in the Jordan, according to the word of the man of God; and his flesh was restored like the flesh of a little child, and he was clean.

Psalm 51:8-13 [page 656]

or this

[Salvation offered freely to all]

A Reading (Lesson) from the Book of Isaiah [55:1-11]

Thus says the Lord: "Ho, every one who thirsts, come to the waters; and he who has no money, come, buy and eat! Come, buy wine and milk without money and without price. Why do you spend your money for that which is not bread, and your labor for that which does not satisfy?

Hearken diligently to me, and eat what is good, and delight yourselves in fatness. Incline your ear, and come to me; hear, that your soul may live; and I will make with you an everlasting covenant, my steadfast, sure love for David. Behold, I made him a witness to the peoples, a leader and commander for the peoples. Behold, you shall call nations that you know not, and nations that knew you not shall run to you, because of the Lord your God, and of the Holy One of Israel, for he has glorified you. Seek the Lord while he may be found, call upon him while he is near; let the wicked forsake his way, and the unrighteous man his thoughts; let him return to the Lord, that he may have mercy on him, and to our God, for he will abundantly pardon. For my thoughts are not your thoughts, neither are your ways my ways, says the Lord. For as the heavens are higher than the earth, so are my ways higher than your ways and my thoughts than your thoughts. For as the rain and the snow come down from heaven, and return not thither but water the earth, making it bring forth and sprout, giving seed to the sower and bread to the eater, so shall my word be that goes forth from my mouth; it shall not return to me empty, but it shall accomplish that which I purpose, and prosper in the thing for which I sent it."

Canticle 9 [page 86]

or this

[A new heart and a new spirit]

A Reading (Lesson) from the Book of Ezekiel
[36:24-28]

Thus says the Lord God: "I will take you from the nations, and gather you from all the countries, and bring you into your own land. I will sprinkle clean water upon you, and you shall be clean from all your uncleannesses, and from all your idols I will cleanse you. A new heart I will give you, and a new spirit I will put within you; and I will take out of your flesh the heart of stone and give you a heart of flesh. And I will put my spirit within you, and cause you to walk in my statutes and be careful to observe my ordinances. You shall dwell in the land which I gave to your fathers; and you shall be my people, and I will be your God."

Psalm 42 [page 643]

or this

[The Spirit of the Lord is upon me]

A Reading (Lesson) from the Book of Isaiah [61:1-9]

The Spirit of the Lord God is upon me, because the Lord has anointed me to bring good tidings to the afflicted; he has sent me to bind up the brokenhearted, to proclaim liberty to the captives, and the opening of the prison to those who are bound; to proclaim the year of the Lord's favor, and the day of vengeance of our God; to comfort all those who mourn; to grant to those who mourn in Zion — to give them a garland instead of ashes, the oil of gladness instead of mourning, the mantle of praise instead of a faint spirit; that they may be called oaks of righteousness, the planting of the Lord, that he may be glorified. They shall build up the ancient ruins, they shall raise up the former devastations; they shall repair the ruined cities, the devastations of many generations. Aliens shall stand and feed your flocks, foreigners shall be your plowmen and vinedressers; but you shall be called the priests of the Lord, men shall speak of you as the ministers of our God; you shall eat the wealth of the nations, and in their riches you shall glory. Instead of your shame you shall have a double portion, instead of dishonor you shall rejoice in your lot; therefore in your land you shall possess a double portion; yours shall be everlasting joy. For I the Lord love justice, I hate robbery and wrong; I will faithfully give them their recompense, and I will make an everlasting covenant with them. Their descendants shall be known among the nations, and their offspring in the midst of the peoples; all who see them shall acknowledge them, that they are a people whom the Lord has blessed.

or this

[Behold my servant]*

A Reading (Lesson) from the Book of Isaiah [42:1-9]

Behold my servant, whom I uphold, my chosen, in whom my soul delights; I have put my Spirit upon him, he will bring forth justice to the nations. He will not cry or lift up his voice, or make it heard in the street; a bruised reed he will not break, and a dimly burning wick he will not quench; he will faithfully bring forth justice. He will not fail or be discouraged till he has established justice in the earth; and the coastlands wait for his law. Thus says God, the Lord, who created the heavens and stretched them out, who spread forth the earth and what comes from it, who gives breath to the people upon it and spirit to those who walk in it: "I am the Lord, I have called you in righteousness, I have taken you by the hand and kept you; I have given you as a covenant to the people, a light to the nations, to open the eyes that are blind, to bring out the

---

**Proper Reading for the Eucharist of the Feast*

prisoners from the dungeon, from the prison those who sit in darkness. I am the Lord, that is my name; my glory I give to no other, nor my praise to graven images. Behold, the former things have come to pass, and new things I now declare; before they spring forth I tell you of them."

Psalm 89:20-29 [page 715]*

or this

FROM THE NEW TESTAMENT

[When God's patience waited in the days of Noah]

A Reading (Lesson) from the First Letter of Peter [3:15b-22]

Always be prepared to make a defense to any one who calls you to account for the hope that is in you, yet do it with gentleness and reverence; and keep your conscience clear, so that, when you are abused, those who revile your good behavior in Christ may be put to shame. For it is better to suffer for doing right, if that should be God's will, than for doing wrong. For Christ also died for sins once for all, the righteous for the unrighteous, that he might bring us to God, being put to death in the flesh but made alive in the spirit; in which he went and preached to the spirits in prison, who formerly did not obey, when God's patience waited in the days of Noah, during the building of the ark, in which a few, that is, eight persons, were saved through water. Baptism, which corresponds to this, now saves you, not as a removal of dirt from the body but as an appeal to God for a clear conscience,

* Proper Psalm for the Eucharist of the Feast

through the resurrection of Jesus Christ, who has gone into heaven and is at the right hand of God, with angels, authorities, and powers subject to him.

or this

[God anointed Jesus with the Holy Spirit]*

A Reading (Lesson) from the Acts of the Apostles [10:34-38]

Peter opened his mouth and said, "Truly I perceive that God shows no partiality, but in every nation any one who fears him and does what is right is acceptable to him. You know the word which he sent to Israel, preaching good news of peace by Jesus Christ (he is Lord of all), the word which was proclaimed throughout all Judea, beginning from Galilee after the baptism which John preached: how God anointed Jesus of Nazareth with the Holy Spirit and with power; how he went about doing good and healing all that were oppressed by the devil, for God was with him."

*Proper Reading for the Eucharist of the Feast

[The Baptism of Jesus]*

YEAR A

✝ *The Holy Gospel of Our Lord Jesus Christ
According to Matthew* [3:13-17]

Jesus came from Galilee to the Jordan to John, to be
baptized by him. John would have prevented him, saying,
"I need to be baptized by you, and do you come to me?"
But Jesus answered him, "Let it be so now; for thus it is
fitting for us to fulfill all righteousness." Then he
consented. And when Jesus was baptized, he went up
immediately from the water, and behold, the heavens were
opened and he saw the Spirit of God descending like a
dove, and alighting on him; and lo, a voice from heaven,
saying, "This is my beloved Son, with whom I am well
pleased."

YEAR B

✝ *The Holy Gospel of Our Lord Jesus Christ
According to Mark* [1:7-11]

John the Baptist preached, saying, "After me comes he
who is mightier than I, the thong of whose sandals I am
not worthy to stoop down and untie. I have baptized you
with water; but he will baptize you with the Holy Spirit."
In those days Jesus came from Nazareth of Galilee and
was baptized by John in the Jordan. And when he came up
out of the water, immediately he saw the heavens opened
and the Spirit descending upon him like a dove; and a
voice came from heaven, "Thou art my beloved Son; with
thee I am well pleased."

*Proper Reading for the Eucharist of the Feast

YEAR C

✝ *The Holy Gospel of Our Lord Jesus Christ According to Luke* [3:15-16,21-22]

As the people were in expectation, and all men questioned in their hearts concerning John, whether perhaps he were the Christ, John answered them all, "I baptize you with water; but he who is mightier than I is coming, the thong of whose sandals I am not worthy to untie; he will baptize you with the Holy Spirit and with fire." Now when all the people were baptized, and when Jesus also had been baptized and was praying, the heaven was opened, and the Holy Spirit descended upon him in bodily form, as a dove, and a voice came from heaven, "Thou art my beloved Son; with thee I am well pleased."

or this

[The resurrection and the great commission]

✝ *The Holy Gospel of Our Lord Jesus Christ According to Matthew* [28:1-10,16-20]

After the sabbath, toward the dawn of the first day of the week, Mary Mag'dalene and the other Mary went to see the sepulchre. And behold, there was a great earthquake; for an angel of the Lord descended from heaven and came and rolled back the stone, and sat upon it. His appearance was like lightning, and his raiment white as snow. And for fear of him the guards trembled and became like dead men. But the angel said to the women, "Do not be afraid; for I know that you seek Jesus who was crucified. He is not here; for he has risen, as he said. Come, see the place where he lay. Then go quickly and tell his disciples that he has risen from the dead, and behold, he is going before you to Galilee; there you will see him. Lo, I have told you." So they departed quickly from the tomb with fear and great joy, and ran to tell his disciples. And behold, Jesus met them and said, "Hail!" And they came up and took hold of his feet and worshiped him. Then Jesus said to them, "Do not be afraid; go and tell my brethren to go to Galilee, and there they will see me." Now the eleven disciples went to Galilee, to the mountain to which Jesus had directed them. And when they saw him they worshiped him; but some doubted. And Jesus came and said to them, "All authority in heaven and on earth has been given to me. Go therefore and make disciples of all nations, baptizing them in the name of the Father and of the Son and of the Holy Spirit, teaching them to observe all that I have commanded you; and lo, I am with you always, to the close of the age."

Rogation Days

At the Procession [BOS, page 101]

In addition to the readings listed on page 930 (for texts see pages 149-155 below) of the Prayer Book, any of the following passages are appropriate:

A Reading (Lesson) from the Book of Genesis [8:13-23]

In the six hundred and first year, in the first month, the first day of the month, the waters were dried from off the earth; and Noah removed the covering of the ark, and looked, and behold, the face of the ground was dry. In the second month, on the twenty-seventh day of the month, the earth was dry. Then God said to Noah, "Go forth from the ark, you and your wife, and your sons and your sons' wives with you. Bring forth with you every living thing that is with you of all flesh — birds and animals and every creeping thing that creeps on the earth, and be fruitful and multiply upon the earth." So Noah went forth, and his sons and his wife and his sons' wives with him. And every beast, every creeping thing, and every bird, everything that moves upon the earth, went forth by families out of the ark. Then Noah built an altar to the Lord, and took of every clean animal and of every clean bird, and offered burnt offerings on the altar. And when the Lord smelled the pleasing odor, the Lord said in his heart, "I will never again curse the ground because of man for the imagination of man's heart is evil from his youth; neither will I ever again destroy every living creature as I have done. While the earth remains, seedtime and harvest, cold and heat, summer and winter, day and night, shall not cease."

or this

A Reading (Lesson) from the Book of Leviticus
[26:1-13(14-20)]

The Lord said to Moses on Mount Sinai, "Say to the people of Israel, you shall make for yourselves no idols and erect no graven image or pillar, and you shall not set up a figured stone in your land, to bow down to them; for I am the Lord your God. You shall keep my sabbaths and reverence my sanctuary: I am the Lord. If you walk in my statutes and observe my commandments and do them, then I will give you your rains in their season, and the land shall yield its increase, and the trees of the field shall yield their fruit. And your threshing shall last to the time of vintage, and the vintage shall last to the time for sowing; and you shall eat your bread to the full, and dwell in your land securely. And I will give peace in the land, and you shall lie down, and none shall make you afraid; and I will remove evil beasts from the land, and the sword shall not go through your land. And you shall chase your enemies, and they shall fall before you by the sword. Five of you shall chase a hundred, a hundred of you shall chase ten thousand; and your enemies shall fall before you by the sword. And I will have regard for you and make you fruitful and multiply you, and will confirm my covenant with you. And you shall eat old store long kept, and you shall clear out the old to make way for the new. And I will make my abode with you, and my soul shall not abhor you. And I will walk among you, and will be your God, and you shall be my people. I am the Lord your God, who brought you forth out of the land of Egypt, that you should not be their slaves; and I have broken the bars of your yoke and made you walk erect."

"But if you will not hearken to me, and will not do all these commandments, if you spurn my statutes, and if your soul abhors my ordinances, so that you will not do all my commandments, but break my covenant, I will do this to you: I will appoint over you sudden terror, consumption, and fever that waste the eyes and cause life to pine away. And you shall sow your seed in vain, for your enemies shall eat it; I will set my face against you, and you shall be smitten before your enemies; those who hate you shall rule over you, and you shall flee when none pursues you. And if in spite of this you will not hearken to me, then I will chastise you again sevenfold for your sins, and I will break the pride of your power, and I will make your heavens like iron and your earth like brass; and your strength shall be spent in vain, for your land shall not yield its increase, and the trees of the land shall not yield their fruit."

or this

A Reading (Lesson) from the Book of Deuteronomy
[8:1-10(11-20)]

Moses said to the people, "All the commandment which I command you this day you shall be careful to do, that you may live and multiply, and go in and possess the land which the Lord swore to give to your fathers. And you shall remember all the ways which the Lord your God has led you these forty years in the wilderness, that he might humble you, testing you to know what was in your heart, whether you would keep his commandments, or not. And he humbled you and let you hunger and fed you with manna, which you did not know, nor did your fathers know; that he might make you know that man does not live by bread alone, but that man lives by everything that proceeds out of the mouth of the Lord. Your clothing did not wear out upon you, and your foot did not swell, these forty years. Know then in your heart that, as a man disciplines his son, the Lord your God disciplines you. So you shall keep the commandments of the Lord your God, by walking in his ways and by fearing him. For the Lord your God is bringing you into a good land, a land of brooks of water, of fountains and springs, flowing forth in valleys and hills, a land of wheat and barley, of vines and fig trees and pomegranates, a land in which you will eat bread without scarcity, in which you will lack nothing, a land whose stones are iron, and out of whose hills you can dig copper. And you shall eat and be full, and you shall bless the Lord your God for the good land he has given you."

"Take heed lest you forget the Lord your God, by not keeping his commandments and his ordinances and his statutes, which I command you this day: lest, when you have eaten and are full, and have built goodly houses and live in them, and when your herds and flocks multiply, and your silver and gold is multiplied, and all that you have is multiplied, then the Lord your God, who brought you out of the land of Egypt, out of the house of bondage, who led you through the great and terrible wilderness, with its fiery serpents and scorpions and thirsty ground where there was no water, who brought you water out of the flinty rock, who fed you in the wilderness with manna which your fathers did not know, that he might humble you and test you, to do you good in the end. Beware lest you say in your heart, 'My power and the might of my hand have gotten me this wealth.' You shall remember the Lord your God, for it is he who gives you power to get wealth; that he may confirm his covenant which he swore to your fathers, as at this day. And if you forget the Lord your God and go after other gods and serve them and worship them, I solemnly warn you this day that you shall surely perish. Like the nations that the Lord makes to perish before you, so shall you perish, because you would not obey the voice of the Lord your God."

or the following

A Reading (Lesson) from the Book of Hosea [2:18-23]

The Lord said, "I will make for you a covenant on that day with the beasts of the field, the birds of the air, and the creeping things of the ground; and I will abolish the bow, the sword, and war from the land; and I will make you lie down in safety. And I will betroth you to me for ever; I will betroth you to me in righteousness and in justice, in steadfast love, and in mercy. I will betroth you to me in faithfulness; and you shall know the Lord. And in that day, says the Lord, I will answer the heavens and they shall answer the earth; and the earth shall answer the grain, the wine, and the oil, and they shall answer Jezreel; and I will sow him for myself in the land. And I will have pity on Not pitied, and I will say to Not my people, 'You are my people': and he shall say, 'Thou art my God.' "

or this

A Reading (Lesson) from the Book of Ezekiel [34:25-31]

"Thus says the Lord God: I will make with them a covenant of peace and banish wild beasts from the land, so that they may dwell securely in the wilderness and sleep in the woods. And I will make them and the places round about my hill a blessing; and I will send down the showers in their season; they shall be showers of blessing. And the trees of the field shall yield their fruit, and the earth shall yield its increase, and they shall be secure in their land; and they shall know that I am the Lord, when I break the bars of their yoke, and deliver them from the hand of those who enslaved them. They shall no more be a prey to the nations, nor shall the beasts of the land devour them; they shall dwell securely, and none shall make them afraid. And I will provide for them prosperous plantations so that they shall no more be consumed with hunger in the land, and no longer suffer the reproach of the nations. And they shall know that I, the Lord their God, am with them, and that they, the house of Israel, are my people, says the Lord God. And you are my sheep, the sheep of my pasture, and I am your God, says the Lord God."

or this

A Reading (Lesson) from the Letter of James [4:7-11]

Submit yourselves to God. Resist the devil and he will flee from you. Draw near to God and he will draw near to you. Cleanse your hands, you sinners, and purify your hearts, you men of double mind. Be wretched and mourn and weep. Let your laughter be turned to mourning and your joy to dejection. Humble yourselves before the Lord and he will exalt you. Do not speak evil against one another, brethren. He that speaks evil against a brother or judges his brothers, speaks evil against the law and judges the law. But if you judge the law, you are not a doer of the law but a judge.

or this

A Reading (Lesson) from the Gospel According to Matthew [6:25-34]

Jesus said, "I tell you, do not be anxious about your life, what you shall eat or what you shall drink, nor about your body, what you shall put on. Is not life more than food, and the body more than clothing? Look at the birds of the air: they neither sow nor reap nor gather into barns, and yet your heavenly Father feeds them. Are you not of more value than they? And which of you by being anxious can add one cubit to his span of life? And why are you anxious about clothing? Consider the lilies of the field, how they grow; they neither toil nor spin; yet I tell you, even Solomon in all his glory was not arrayed like one of these.

But if God so clothes the grass of the field, which today is alive and tomorrow is thrown into the oven, will he not much more clothe you, O men of little faith? Therefore do not be anxious, saying 'What shall we eat?' or 'What shall we drink?' or 'What shall we wear?' For the Gentiles seek all these things; and your heavenly Father knows that you need them all. But seek first his kingdom and his righteousness, and all these things shall be yours as well. Therefore do not be anxious about tomorrow, for tomorrow will be anxious for itself. Let the day's own trouble be sufficient for the day."

or this

A Reading (Lesson) from the Gospel According to John [12:23-26]

Jesus said to Andrew and Philip, "The hour has come for the Son of man to be glorified. Truly, truly, I say to you, unless a grain of wheat falls into the earth and dies, it remains alone; but if it dies, it bears much fruit. He who loves his life loses it, and he who hates his life in this world will keep it for eternal life. If any one serves me, he must follow me; and where I am, there shall my servant be also; if any one serves me, the Father will honor him."

Propers for the Eucharist

[BCP, Various Occasions, Proper 19, page 930]

For Rogation Days I

A Reading (Lesson) from the Book of Deuteronomy
[11:10-15]

Moses said to the people, "The land which you are entering to take possession of it is not like the land of Egypt, from which you have come, where you sowed your seed and watered it with your feet, like a garden of vegetables; but the land which you are going over to possess is a land of hills and valleys, which drinks water by the rain from heaven, a land which the Lord your God cares for; the eyes of the Lord your God are always upon it, from the beginning of the year to the end of the year. And if you will obey my commandments which I command you this day, to love the Lord your God, and to serve him with all your heart and with all your soul, he will give the rain for your land in its season, the early rain and the later rain, that you may gather in your grain and your wine and your oil. And he will give grass in your fields for your cattle, and you shall eat and be full."

or this

A Reading (Lesson) from the Book of Ezekiel [47:6-12]

The Lord said to me, "Son of man, have you seen this?" Then he led me back along the bank of the river. As I went back, I saw upon the bank of the river very many trees on the one side and on the other. And he said to me, "This water flows toward the eastern region and goes down into the Arabah; and when it enters the stagnant waters of the sea, the water will become fresh. And wherever the river goes every living creature which swarms will live, and there will be very many fish; for this water goes there, that the waters of the sea may become fresh; so everything will live where the river goes. Fishermen will stand beside the sea; from En-ge'di to En-eg'laim it will be a place for the spreading of nets; its fish will be of very many kinds, like the fish of the Great Sea. But its swamps and marshes will not become fresh; they are to be left for salt. And on the banks, on both sides of the river, there will grow all kinds of trees for food. Their leaves will not wither nor their fruit fail, but they will bear fresh fruit every month, because the water for them flows from the sanctuary. Their fruit will be for food, and their leaves for healing."

or this

A Reading (Lesson) from the Book of Jeremiah [14:1-9]

The word of the Lord which came to Jeremiah concerning the drought: "Judah mourns and her gates languish; her people lament on the ground, and the cry of Jerusalem goes up. Her nobles send their servants for water; they come to the cisterns, they find no water, they return with their vessels empty; they are ashamed and confounded and cover their heads. Because of the ground which is dismayed, since there is no rain on the land, the farmers are ashamed, they cover their heads. Even the hind in the field forsakes her new born calf because there is no grass. The wild asses stand on the bare heights, they pant for air like jackals; their eyes fail because there is no herbage. Though our iniquities testify against us, act O Lord, for thy name's sake; for our backslidings are many, we have sinned against thee. O thou hope of Israel, its savior in time of trouble, why shouldst thou be like a stranger in the land, like a wayfarer who turns aside to tarry for a night?

Why shouldst thou be like a man confused, like a mighty man who cannot save? Yet thou, O Lord, art in the midst of us, and we are called by thy name; leave us not."

Psalm 147 [page 804]   or   *Psalm 147:1-13* [page 804]

A Reading (Lesson) from the Letter of Paul to the Romans [8:18-25]

I consider that the sufferings of this present time are not worth comparing with the glory that is to be revealed to us. For the creation waits with eager longing for the revealing of the sons of God; for the creation was subjected to futility, not of its own will but by the will of him who subjected it in hope; because the creation itself will be set free from its bondage to decay and obtain the glorious liberty of the children of God. We know that the whole creation has been groaning in travail together until now; and not only the creation, but we ourselves, who have the first fruits of the Spirit, groan inwardly as we wait for adoption as sons, the redemption of our bodies. For in this hope we were saved. Now hope that is seen is not hope. For who hopes for what he sees? But if we hope for what we do not see, we wait for it with patience.

✝ *The Holy Gospel of Our Lord Jesus Christ According to Mark* [4:26-32]

Jesus said, "The kingdom of God is as if a man should scatter seed upon the ground, and should sleep and rise night and day, and the seed should sprout and grow, he knows not how. The earth produces of itself, first the blade, then the ear, then the full grain in the ear. But when the grain is ripe, at once he puts in the sickle, because the harvest has come." And he said, "With what can we compare the kingdom of God, or what parable shall we use for it? It is like a grain of mustard seed, which, when sown upon the ground, is the smallest of all the seeds on earth; yet when it is sown it grows up and becomes the greatest of all shrubs, and puts forth large branches, so that the birds of the air can make nests in its shade."

For Rogation Days II

A Reading (Lesson) from the Book of Ecclesiasticus [38:27-32]

So too is every craftsman and master workman who labors by night as well as by day; those who cut the signets of seals, each is diligent in making a great variety; he sets his heart on painting a lifelike image, and he is careful to finish his work. So too is the smith sitting by the anvil, intent upon his handiwork in iron; the breath of the fire melts his flesh, and he wastes away in the heat of the furnace; he inclines his ear to the sound of the hammer, and his eyes are on the pattern of the object. He sets his heart on finishing his handiwork, and he is careful to complete his decoration. So too is the potter sitting at his work and turning the wheel with his feet; he is always deeply concerned over his work, and his output is by number. He molds the clay with his arm and makes it pliable with his feet; he sets his heart to finish the glazing, and he is careful to clean the furnace All these rely upon their hands, and each is skilful in his own work. Without them a city cannot be established, and men can neither sojourn nor live there.

Psalm 107:1-9 [page 746]

A Reading (Lesson) from the First Letter of Paul to the Corinthians [3:10-14]

According to the grace of God given to me, like a skilled master builder I laid a foundation, and another man is building upon it. Let each man take care how he builds upon it. For no other foundation can any one lay than that which is laid, which is Jesus Christ. Now if any one builds on the foundation with gold, silver, precious stones, wood, hay, straw—each man's work will become manifest; for the Day will disclose it, because it will be revealed with fire, and the fire will test what sort of work each one has done. If the work which any man has built on the foundation survives, he will receive a reward.

✝ *The Holy Gospel of Our Lord Jesus Christ According to Matthew* [6:19-24]

Jesus said, "Do not lay up for yourselves treasures on earth, where moth and rust consume and where thieves break in and steal, but lay up for yourselves treasure in heaven, where neither moth nor rust consumes and where thieves do not break in and steal. For where your treasure is, there will your heart be also. The eye is the lamp of the body. So, if your eye is sound, your whole body will be full of light; but if your eye is not sound, your whole body will be full of darkness. If then the light in you is darkness, how great is the darkness! No one can serve two masters; for either he will hate the one and love the other, or he will be devoted to the one and despise the other. You cannot serve God and mammon."

For Rogation Days III

A Reading (Lesson) from the Book of Job [38:1-11,16-18]

Then the Lord answered Job out of the whirlwind: "Who is this that darkens counsel by words without knowledge? Gird up your loins like a man, I will question you, and you shall declare to me. Where were you when I laid the foundation of the earth? Tell me, if you have

understanding. Who determined its measurements —
surely you know! Or who stretched the line upon it? On
what were its bases sunk, or who laid its cornerstone,
when the morning stars sang together, and all the sons of
God shouted for joy? Or who shut in the sea with doors,
when it burst forth from the womb; when I made the
clouds its garment, and thick darkness its swaddling band,
and prescribed bounds for it, and set bars and doors, and
said, 'Thus far shall you come, and no farther, and here
shall your proud waves be stayed'? Have you entered into
the springs of the sea, or walked in the recesses of the
deep? Have the gates of death been revealed to you, or
have you seen the gates of deep darkness? Have you
comprehended the expanse of the earth? Declare, if you
know all this."

Psalm 104:25-37 [page 736]   or

Psalm 104:1,13-15,25-32 [page 735]

*A Reading (Lesson) from the First Letter of Paul
to Timothy* [6:7-10,17-19]

We brought nothing into the world, and we cannot take
anything out of the world; but if we have food and
clothing, with these we shall be content. But those who
desire to be rich fall into temptation, into a snare, into
many senseless and hurtful desires that plunge men into
ruin and destruction. For the love of money is the root of
all evils; it is through this craving that some have
wandered away from the faith and pierced their hearts
with many pangs. As for the rich in this world, charge
them not to be haughty, nor to set their hopes on
uncertain riches but on God who richly furnishes us with
everything to enjoy. They are to do good, to be rich in

154   *For Rogation Days III*

good deeds, liberal and generous, thus laying up for themselves a good foundation for the future, so that they may take hold of the life which is life indeed.

✝ *The Holy Gospel of Our Lord Jesus Christ According to Luke* [12:13-21]

One of the multitude said to Jesus, "Teacher, bid my brother to divide the inheritance with me." But he said to him, "Man, who made me a judge or divider over you?" And he said to them, "Take heed, and beware of all covetousness; for a man's life does not consist in the abundance of his possessions." And he told them a parable, saying, "The land of a rich man brought forth plentifully; and he thought to himself, 'What shall I do, for I have nowhere to store my crops?' And he said, 'I will do this: I will pull down my barns, and build large ones; and there I will store all my grain and my goods. And I will say to my soul, Soul, you have ample goods laid up for many years; take your ease, eat, drink, be merry.' But God said to him, 'Fool! This night your soul is required of you; and the things you have prepared, whose will they be?' So is he who lays up treasure for himself, and is not rich toward God."

Vigil for the Eve of All Saints' Day
or the Sunday after All Saints' Day
[BOS, page 104]

For use with a Baptismal Vigil of All Saints in accordance with the rubrics.

[The call of Abraham]

A Reading (Lesson) from the Book of Genesis [12:1-8]

The Lord said to Abram, "Go from your country and your kindred and your father's house to the land that I will show you. And I will make of you a great nation, and I will bless you, and make your name great, so that you will be a blessing. I will bless those who bless you, and him who curses you I will curse; and by you all the families of the earth shall bless themselves." So Abram went, as the Lord had told him; and Lot went with him. Abram was seventy-five years old when he departed from Haran. And Abram took Sar'ai his wife, and Lot his brother's son, and all their possessions which they had gathered, and the persons that they had gotten in Haran; and they set forth to go to the land of Canaan. When they had come to the land of Canaan, Abram passed through the land to the place at Shechem, to the oak of Moreh. At that time the Canaanites were in the land. Then the Lord appeared to Abram, and said, "To your descendants I will give this land." So he built there an altar to the Lord, who had appeared to him. Thence he removed to the mountain on the east of Bethel, and pitched his tent, with Bethel on the west and Ai on the east; and there he built an altar to the Lord and called on the name of the Lord.

Psalm 113 [page 756]

or this

[Daniel delivered from the lions' den]

A Reading (Lesson) from the Book of Daniel [6:(1-15)16-23]

It pleased Darius to set over the kingdom a hundred and twenty satraps, to be throughout the whole kingdom; and over them three presidents, of whom Daniel was one, to whom these satraps should give account, so that the king might suffer no loss. Then this Daniel became distinguished above all the other presidents and satraps, because an excellent spirit was in him; and the king planned to set him over the whole kingdom. Then the presidents and the satraps sought to find a ground for complaint against Daniel with regard to the kingdom; but they could find no ground for complaint or any fault, because he was faithful, and no error or fault was found in him. Then these men said, "We shall not find any ground for complaint against this Daniel unless we find it in connection with the law of God." Then these presidents and satraps came by agreement to the king and said to him, "O King Darius, live for ever! All the presidents of the kingdom, the prefects and the satraps, the counselors and the governors are agreed that the king should establish an ordinance and enforce an interdict, that whoever makes petition to any god or man for thirty days, except to you, O king, shall be cast into the den of lions. Now, O king, establish the interdict and sign the document, so that it cannot be changed, according to the law of the Medes and the Persians, which cannot be revoked." When Daniel knew that the document had been signed, he went to his house where he had windows in his upper chamber open toward Jerusalem; and he got down upon his knees three times a day and prayed and gave thanks before his God, as he had done previously. Then these men came by agreement and found Daniel making petition and supplication before his God. Then they came near and said before the king, concerning the interdict, "O king! Did you not sign an interdict, that any man who makes petition to any god or man within thirty days except to you, O king, shall be cast into the den of lions?" The king answered, "The thing stands fast, according to the law of the Medes and Persians, which cannot be revoked." Then they answered before the king, "That Daniel, who is one of the exiles from Judah, pays no heed to you, O king, or the interdict you have signed, but makes his petition three times a day." Then the king, when he heard these words, was much distressed, and set his mind to deliver Daniel; and he labored till the sun went down to rescue him. Then these men came by agreement to the king, and said to the king, "Know, O king, that it is a law of the Medes and Persians that no interdict or ordinance which the king establishes can be changed."

[Because Daniel had broken the interdict of Darius, the king of Babylon, which forbade petition to any god or man except the king]
Darius commanded, and Daniel was brought and cast into the den of lions. The king said to Daniel, "May your God, whom you serve continually, deliver you!" And a stone was brought and laid upon the mouth of the den, and the king sealed it with his own signet and with the signet of

his lords, that nothing might be changed concerning Daniel. Then the king went to his palace, and spent the night fasting; no diversions were brought to him, and sleep fled from him. Then, at break of day, the king arose and went in haste to the den of lions. When he came near to the den where Daniel was, he cried out in a tone of anguish and said to Daniel, "O Daniel, servant of the living God, has your God, whom you serve continually, been able to deliver you from the lions?" Then Daniel said to the king, "O king, live for ever! My God sent his angel and shut the lions' mouths, and they have not hurt me, because I was found blameless before him; and also before you, O king, I have done no wrong." Then the king was exceedingly glad and commanded that Daniel be taken up out of the den. So Daniel was taken up out of the den, and no kind of hurt was found upon him, because he had trusted in his God.

Canticle 2 [page 49]   or   *Canticle 13* [page 90]

or this

[The testament and death of Mattathi′as]

A Reading (Lesson) from the First Book of the Maccabees [2:49-64]

The days drew near for Mattathi′as to die, and he said to his sons: "Arrogance and reproach have now become strong, it is a time of ruin and furious anger. Now, my children, show zeal for the law, and give your lives for the covenant of our fathers. Remember the deeds of the fathers, which they did in their generations; and receive great honor and an everlasting name. Was not Abraham found faithful when tested, and it was reckoned to him as righteousness? Joseph in the time of his distress kept the commandment, and became lord of Egypt. Phin'ehas our father, because he was deeply zealous, received the covenant of everlasting priesthood. Joshua, because he fulfilled the command, became a judge in Israel. Caleb, because he testified in the assembly, received an inheritance in the land. David, because he was merciful, inherited the throne of the kingdom for ever. Eli'jah because of great zeal for the law was taken up into heaven. Hanani'ah, Azari'ah and Mish'a-el believed and were saved from the flame. Daniel because of his innocence was delivered from the mouth of the lions. And so observe, from generation to generation, that none who put their trust in him will lack stength. Do not fear the words of a sinner, for his splendor will turn into dung and worms. Today he will be exalted, but tomorrow he will not be found, because he has returned to the dust, and his plans will perish. My children, be courageous and grow strong in the law, for by it you will gain honor."

Psalm 1 [page 585]

or this

[The martyrdom of the seven brothers]

A Reading (Lesson) from the Second Book of the Maccabees [6:1-2;7:1-23]

Anti'ochus the king sent an Athenian senator to compel the Jews to forsake the laws of their fathers and cease to live by the laws of God, and also to pollute the temple in Jerusalem and call it the temple of Olympian Zeus, and to call the one in Ger'izim the temple of Zeus the Friend of Strangers, as did the people who dwelt in that place. It happened also that seven brothers and their mother were arrested and were being compelled by the king, under torture with whips and cords, to partake of unlawful swine's flesh. One of them, acting as their spokesman, said, "What do you intend to ask and learn from us? For we are ready to die rather than transgress the laws of our fathers." The king fell into a rage, and gave orders that pans and caldrons be heated. These were heated immediately, and he commanded that the tongue of their spokesman be cut out and that they scalp him and cut off his hands and feet, while the rest of the brothers and the mother looked on. When he was utterly helpless, the king ordered them to take him to the fire, still breathing, and to fry him in a pan. The smoke from the pan spread widely, but the brothers and their mother encouraged one another to die nobly, saying, "The Lord God is watching over us and in truth has compassion on us, as Moses declared in his song which bore witness against the people to their faces, when he said, 'And he will have compassion on his servants.' " After the first brother had died in this way, they brought forward the second for their sport. They tore off the skin of his head with the hair, and asked him, "Will you eat rather than have your body punished limb by limb?" He replied in the language of his fathers, and said to them, "No." Therefore he in turn underwent tortures as the first brother had done. And when he was at his last breath, he said, "You accursed wretch, you dismiss us from this present life, but the King of the universe will raise us up to an everlasting renewal of life, because we have died for his laws." After him, the third was the victim of their sport. When it was demanded, he quickly put out his tongue and courageously stretched forth his hands, and said nobly "I got these from Heaven, and because of his laws I disdain them, and from him I hope to get them back again." As a result the king himself and those with him were astonished at the young man's spirit, for he regarded his sufferings as nothing. When he too had died, they maltreated and tortured the fourth in the same way. And when he was near death, he said, "One cannot but choose to die at the hands of men and to cherish the hope that God gives of being raised again by him. But for you there will be no resurrection to life!" Next they brought forward the fifth and maltreated him. But he looked at the king, and said, "Because you have authority among men, mortal though you are, you do what you please. But do not think that God has forsaken our people. Keep on, and see how his mighty power will torture you and your descendants!" After him they brought forward the sixth. And when he was about to die, he said, "Do not deceive yourself in vain. For we are suffering these things on our own account, because of our sins against our God. Therefore astounding things have happened. But do not think that you will go unpunished for having tried to fight against God!" The mother was especially admirable and worthy of honorable memory. Though she saw her seven sons perish within a single day, she bore it with good courage because of her hope in the Lord. She encouraged each of them in the language of their fathers. Filled with a noble spirit, she fired her woman's reasoning with a man's courage, and said to them, "I do not know how you came into being in my womb. It was not I who gave you life and breath, nor I who set in order the elements within each of you. Therefore the Creator of the world, who shaped the beginning of man and devised the origin of all things, will in his mercy give life and breath back to you again, since you now forget yourselves for the sake of his laws."

Psalm 111 [page 754]

or this

[The eulogy of the ancestors] *

A Reading (Lesson) from the Book of Ecclesiasticus
[44:1-10,13-14]

Let us now praise famous men, and our fathers in their generations. The Lord apportioned to them great glory, his majesty from the beginning. There were those who ruled in their kingdoms, and were men renowned for their power, giving counsel by their understanding, and proclaiming prophecies; leaders of the people in their deliberations and in understanding of learning for the people, wise in their words of instruction; those who composed musical tunes, and set forth verses in writing; rich men furnished with resources, living peaceably in their habitations—all these were honored in their generations, and were the glory of their times. There are some of them who have left a name, so that men declare their praise. And there are some who have no memorial, who have perished as though they had not lived; they have become as though they had not been born, and so have their children after them. But these were men of mercy, whose righteous deeds have not been forgotten; their posterity will continue for ever, and their glory will not be blotted out. Their bodies were buried in peace, and their name lives to all generations.

Psalm 116 [page 759]

or the following

*Proper Reading for the Eucharist of All Saints.

[Surrounded by a great cloud of witnesses]*

A Reading (Lesson) from the Letter to the Hebrews
[11:32(33-38)39—12:2]

What more shall I say? For time would fail me to tell of Gideon, Barak, Samson, Jephthah, of David and Samuel and the prophets—

> who through faith conquered kingdoms, enforced justice, received promises, stopped the mouths of lions, quenched raging fire, escaped the edge of the sword, won strength out of weakness, became mighty in war, put foreign armies to flight. Women received their dead by resurrection. Some were tortured, refusing to accept release, that they might rise again to a better life. Others suffered mocking and scourging, and even chains and imprisonment. They were stoned, they were sawn in two, they were killed with the sword; they went about in skins of sheep and goats, destitute, afflicted, ill-treated—of whom the world was not worthy—wandering over deserts and mountains, and in dens and caves of the earth.

For all these, though well attested by their faith, did not receive what was promised, since God had foreseen something better for us, that apart from us they should not be made perfect. Therefore, since we are surrounded by so great a cloud of witnesses, let us also lay aside every weight, and sin which clings so closely, and let us run with perseverance the race that is set before us, looking to Jesus

*Appointed also for Morning Prayer on All Saints' Day.

the pioneer and perfecter of our faith, who for the joy that was set before him endured the cross, despising the shame, and is seated at the right hand of the throne of God.

Psalm 149 [page 807]*

or this

[The reward of the Saints]*

A Reading (Lesson) from the Revelation to John [7:2-4,9-17]

I saw another angel ascend from the rising of the sun, with the seal of the living God, and he called with a loud voice to the four angels who had been given power to harm earth and sea, saying, "Do not harm the earth or the sea or the trees, till we have sealed the servants of our God upon their foreheads." And I heard the number of the sealed, a hundred and forty-four thousand sealed, out of every tribe of the sons of Israel. After this I looked, and behold, a great multitude which no man could number, from every nation, from all tribes and peoples and tongues, standing before the throne and before the Lamb, clothed in white robes, with palm branches in their hands, and crying out with a loud voice, "Salvation belongs to our God who sits upon the throne, and to the Lamb!" And all the angels stood round the throne and round the elders and the four living creatures, and they fell on their faces before the throne and worshiped God, saying, "Amen! Blessing and glory and wisdom and thanksgiving and honor and power and might be to our God for ever and ever! Amen." Then one of the elders addressed me, saying,

*Proper Reading and Psalm for the Eucharist of All Saints.

"Who are these, clothed in white robes, and whence have they come?" I said to him, "Sir, you know." And he said to me, "These are they who have come out of the great tribulation; they have washed their robes and made them white in the blood of the Lamb. Therefore are they before the throne of God, and serve him day and night within his temple; and he who sits upon the throne will shelter them with his presence. They shall hunger no more, neither thirst any more; the sun shall not strike them, nor any scorching heat. For the Lamb in the midst of the throne will be their shepherd, and he will guide them to springs of living water; and God will wipe away every tear from their eyes."

[The Beatitudes]*

✝ *The Holy Gospel of Our Lord Jesus Christ According to Matthew* [5:1-12]

Seeing the crowds, Jesus went up on the mountain, and when he sat down his disciples came to him. And he opened his mouth and taught them, saying: "Blessed are the poor in spirit, for theirs is the kingdom of heaven. Blessed are those who mourn, for they shall be comforted. Blessed are the meek, for they shall inherit the earth. Blessed are those who hunger and thirst for righteousness, for they shall be satisfied. Blessed are the merciful, for they shall obtain mercy. Blessed are the pure in heart, for they shall see God. Blessed are the peacemakers, for they shall be called sons of God. Blessed are those who are persecuted for righteousness' sake, for theirs is the kingdom of heaven. Blessed are you when men revile you and persecute you and utter all kinds of evil against you

*Proper Reading for the Eucharist of All Saints.

166 *All Saints' Day*

falsely on my account. Rejoice and be glad, for your reward is great in heaven, for so men persecuted the prophets who were before you."

or this

["I will give you rest"]

✝ *The Holy Gospel of Our Lord Jesus Christ According to Matthew* [11:27-30]

Jesus said, "All things have been delivered to me by my Father; and no one knows the Son except the Father, and no one knows the Father except the Son and any one to whom the Son chooses to reveal him. Come to me, all who labor and are heavy laden, and I will give you rest. Take my yoke upon you, and learn from me; for I am gentle and lowly in heart, and you will find rest for your souls. For my yoke is easy, and my burden is light."

or this

[The resurrection and the great commission]*

✝ *The Holy Gospel of Our Lord Jesus Christ According to Matthew* [28:1-10,16-20]

After the sabbath, toward the dawn of the first day of the week, Mary Mag'dalene and the other Mary went to see the sepulchre. And behold, there was a great earthquake; for an angel of the Lord descended from heaven and came and rolled back the stone, and sat upon it. His appearance was like lightning, and his raiment white as snow. And for

On Saturday evening only.

fear of him the guards trembled and became like dead men. But the angel said to the women, "Do not be afraid; for I know that you seek Jesus who was crucified. He is not here; for he has risen, as he said. Come, see the place where he lay. Then go quickly and tell his disciples that he has risen from the dead, and behold, he is going before you to Galilee; there you will see him. Lo, I have told you." So they departed quickly from the tomb with fear and great joy, and ran to tell his disciples. And behold, Jesus met them and said, "Hail!" And they came up and took hold of his feet and worshiped him. Then Jesus said to them, "Do not be afraid; go and tell my brethren to go to Galilee, and there they will see me." Now the eleven disciples went to Galilee, to the mountain to which Jesus had directed them. And when they saw him they worshiped him; but some doubted. And Jesus came and said to them, "All authority in heaven and on earth has been given to me. Go therefore and make disciples of all nations, baptizing them in the name of the Father and of the Son and of the Holy Spirit, teaching them to observe all that I have commanded you; and lo, I am with you always, to the close of the age."

Service for All Hallows' Eve
[BOS, page 106]

This service may be used on the evening of October 31, in accordance with the rubrics and suggestions.

[The witch of Endor]

(It is appropriate that this lesson be read by a narrator, and by other readers for Saul, the witch, and Samuel.)

A Reading (Lesson) from the First Book of Samuel
[28:3-25]

Samuel had died, and all Israel had mourned for him and buried him in Ramah, his own city. And Saul had put the mediums and the wizards out of the land. The Philistines assembled, and came and encamped at Shunem; and Saul gathered all Israel, and they encamped at Gilbo'a. When Saul saw the army of the Philistines, he was afraid, and his heart trembled greatly. And when Saul inquired of the Lord, the Lord did not answer him, either by dreams, or by Urim, or by prophets. Then Saul said to his servants, "Seek out for me a woman who is a medium, that I may go to her and inquire of her." And his servants said to him, "Behold, there is a medium at Endor." So Saul disguised himself and put on other garments, and went, he and two men with him; and they came to the woman by night. And he said, "Divine for me by a spirit, and bring up for me whomever I shall name to you." The woman said to him, "Surely you know what Saul has done, how he has cut off the mediums and the wizards from the land. Why then are you laying a snare for my life to bring about my death?" But Saul swore to her by the Lord, "As the Lord lives, no punishment shall come upon you for this thing." Then the woman said, "Whom shall I bring up for you?" He said, "Bring up Samuel for me." When the woman saw Samuel, she cried out with a loud voice; and the woman said to Saul, "Why have you deceived me? You are Saul." The king said to her, "Have no fear; what do you see?" And the woman said to Saul, "I see a god coming up out of the earth." He said to her, "What is his appearance?" And she said, "An old man is coming up; and he is wrapped in a robe." And Saul knew that it was Samuel, and he bowed with his face to the ground, and did obeisance. Then Samuel said to Saul, "Why have you disturbed me by bringing me up?" Saul answered, "I am in great distress; for the Philistines are warring against me, and God has turned away from me and answers me no more, either by prophets or by dreams; therefore I have summoned you to tell me what I shall do." And Samuel said, "Why then do you ask me, since the Lord has turned from you and become your enemy? The Lord has done to you as he spoke by me; for the Lord has torn the kingdom out of your hand, and given it to your neighbor, David. Because you did not obey the voice of the Lord, and did not carry out his fierce wrath against Am'alek, therefore the Lord has done this thing to you this day. Moreover the Lord will give Israel also with you into the hand of the Philistines; and tomorrow you and your sons shall be with me; the Lord will give the army of Israel also into the hand of the Philistines." Then Saul fell at once full length upon the ground, filled with fear because of the words of Samuel; and there was no strength in him, for he had eaten nothing all day and all night. And the woman came to Saul, and said to him, "Behold, your handmaid has hearkened to you; I have taken my life in my hand, and have hearkened to what you have said to me. Now therefore, you also hearken to your handmaid; let me set a morsel of bread before you; and eat, that you may have strength when you go on your way." He refused, and said, "I will not eat." But his servants, together with the woman, urged him; and he hearkened to their words. So he arose from the earth, and sat upon the bed. Now the woman had a fatted calf in the house, and she quickly killed it, and she took flour, and kneaded it and baked unleavened bread of it, and she put it before Saul and his servants; and they ate. Then they rose and went away that night.

Psalm 130 [page 784]

[The vision of El'iphaz the Te'manite]*

A Reading (Lesson) from the Book of Job [4:12-21]

El'iphaz the Te'manite said to Job, "A word was brought to me stealthily, my ear received the whisper of it. Amid thoughts from visions of the night, when deep sleep falls on men, dread came upon me, and trembling, which made all my bones shake. A spirit glided past my face; the hair of my flesh stood up. It stood still, but I could not discern its appearance. A form was before my eyes; there was silence, then I heard a voice: 'Can mortal man be righteous before God? Can a man be pure before his Maker? Even in his servants he puts no trust, and his angels he charges with error; how much more those who dwell in houses of clay, whose foundation is in the dust, who are crushed before the moth. Between morning and evening they are destroyed; they perish for ever without any regarding it. If their tent-cord is plucked up within them, do they not die, and that without wisdom?' "

Psalm 13 [page 597]   or   *Psalm 108:1-6* [page 749]

[The valley of dry bones]

A Reading (Lesson) from the Book of Ezekiel
[37:1-14]

The hand of the Lord was upon me, and he brought me out by the Spirit of the Lord, and set me down in the midst of the valley; it was full of bones. And he led me round among them; and behold, there were very many upon the valley; and lo, they were very dry. And he said to me, "Son of man, can these bones live?" And I answered, "O Lord God, thou knowest." Again he said to me, "Prophesy to these bones, and say to them, O dry bones, hear the word of the Lord. Thus says the Lord God to these bones: Behold, I will cause breath to enter you, and you shall live. And I will lay sinews upon you, and will cause flesh to come upon you, and cover you with skin, and put breath in you, and you shall live; and you shall know that I am the Lord." So I prophesied as I was commanded; and as I prophesied, there was a noise, and behold, a rattling; and the bones came together, bone to its bone. And as I looked, there were sinews on them, and the flesh had come upon them, and skin had covered them; but there was no breath in them. Then he said to me, "Prophesy to the breath, prophesy, son of man, and say to the breath, Thus says the Lord God: Come from the four winds, O breath, and breathe upon these slain, that they may live." So I prophesied as he commanded me, and the breath came into them, and they lived, and stood upon their feet, an exceedingly great host. Then he said to me, "Son of man, these bones are the whole house of Israel. Behold, they say, 'Our bones are dried up, and our hope is lost; we are clean cut off.' Therefore prophesy, and say to them, Thus says the Lord God: Behold, I will open your graves, and raise you from your graves, O my people; and I will bring you home into the land of Israel. And you shall know that I am the Lord, when I open your graves, and raise you from your graves, O my people. And I will put my Spirit within you, and you shall live, and I will place you in your own land; then you shall know that I, the Lord, have spoken, and I have done it, says the Lord."

Psalm 143:1-11 [page 798]

[The war in heaven]

A Reading (Lesson) from the Revelation to John
[12:(1-6)7-12]

A great portent appeared in heaven, a woman clothed with the sun, with the moon under her feet, and on her head a crown of twelve stars; she was with child and she cried out in her pangs of birth, in anguish for delivery. Another portent appeared in heaven; behold, a great red dragon with seven heads and ten horns, and seven diadems upon his heads. His tail swept down a third of the stars of heaven, and cast them to the earth. And the dragon stood before the woman who was about to bear a child, that he might devour her child when she brought it forth; she brought forth a male child, one who is to rule all the nations with a rod of iron, but her child was caught up to God and to his throne, and the woman fled into the wilderness, where she has a place prepared by God, in which to be nourished for one thousand two hundred and sixty days.

Now war arose in heaven, Michael and his angels fighting against the dragon; and the dragon and his angels fought, but they were defeated and there was no longer any place for them in heaven. And the great dragon was thrown down, that ancient serpent, who is called the Devil and Satan, the deceiver of the whole world—he was thrown down to the earth, and his angels were thrown down with him. And I heard a loud voice in heaven, saying, "Now the salvation and the power and the kingdom of our God and the authority of his Christ have come, for the accuser of our brethren has been thrown down, who accuses them day and night before our God. And they have conquered him by the blood of the Lamb and by the word of their testimony; for they loved not their lives even unto death. Rejoice then, O heaven and you that dwell therein! But woe to you, O earth and sea, for the devil has come down to you in great wrath, because he knows that his time is short!"

Psalm 103:17-22 [page 734] or

Canticle 1 (parts I & IV) [page 47] or

Canticle 12 (Invocation, Part III, Doxology) [page 88]

Celebration for a Home

[BOS, page 131]

One or both of the following Lessons, or other appropriate Readings, may be read:

A Reading (Lesson) from the Book of Genesis [18:1-8]

The Lord appeared to Abraham by the oaks of Mamre, as he sat at the door of his tent in the heat of the day. He lifted up his eyes and looked, and behold, three men stood in front of him. When he saw them, he ran from the tent door to meet them, and bowed himself to the earth, and said, "My lord, if I have found favor in your sight, do not pass by your servant. Let a little water be brought, and wash your feet, and rest yourselves under the tree, while I fetch a morsel of bread, that you may refresh yourselves, and after that you may pass on—since you have come to your servant." So they said, "Do as you have said." And Abraham hastened into the tent to Sarah, and said, "Make ready quickly three measures of fine meal, knead it, and make cakes." And Abraham ran to the herd, and took a calf, tender and good, and gave it to the servant, who hastened to prepare it. Then he took curds, and milk, and the calf which he had prepared, and set it before them; and he stood by them under the tree while they ate.

A Reading (Lesson) from the Third Letter of John [1-6a,11,13-15]

The elder to the beloved Ga'ius, whom I love in the truth. Beloved, I pray that all may go well with you and that you may be in health, I know that it is well with your soul. For

I greatly rejoiced when some of the brethren arrived and testified to the truth of your life, as indeed you do follow the truth. No greater joy can I have than this, to hear that my children follow the truth. Beloved, it is a loyal thing you do when you render any service to the brethren, especially to strangers, who have testified to your love before the church. Beloved, do not imitate evil but imitate good. He who does good is of God; he who does evil has not seen God. I had much to write to you, but I would rather not write with pen and ink; I hope to see you soon, and we will talk together face to face. Peace be to you. The friends greet you. Greet the friends, every one of them.

Between the Readings, or after the Reading if only one is used, Psalm 112:1-7 [page 755], or some other psalm or song, may be sung or said.

If there is to be a Communion, a passage from the Gospel is always included. The following are appropriate:

✝ *The Holy Gospel of Our Lord Jesus Christ According to John* [11:5;12:1-3]

Jesus loved Martha and her sister and Laz'arus. Six days before the Passover, Jesus came to Bethany, where Laz'arus was, whom Jesus had raised from the dead. There they made him a supper; Martha served, and Laz'arus was one of those at table with him. Mary took a pound of costly ointment of pure nard and anointed the feet of Jesus and wiped his feet with her hair; and the house was filled with the fragrance of the ointment.

or this

✝ *The Holy Gospel of Our Lord Jesus Christ According to Matthew* [6:25-33]

Jesus said, "Therefore I tell you, do not be anxious about your life, what you shall eat or what you shall drink, nor about your body, what you shall put on. Is not life more than food, and the body more than clothing? Look at the birds of the air: they neither sow nor reap nor gather into barns, and yet your heavenly Father feeds them. Are you not of more value than they? And which of you by being anxious can add one cubit to his span of life? And why are you anxious about clothing? Consider the lilies of the field, how they grow; they neither toil nor spin; yet I tell you, even Solomon in all his glory was not arrayed like one of these. But if God so clothes the grass of the field, which today is alive and tomorrow is thrown into the oven, will he not much more clothe you, O men of little faith? Therefore do not be anxious, saying, 'What shall we eat?' or 'What shall we drink?' or 'What shall we wear?' For the Gentiles seek all these things; and your heavenly Father knows that you need them all. But seek first his kingdom and his righteousness, and all these things shall be yours as well."

Commissioning for Lay Ministries in the Church

[BOS, page 176]

When used as a separate service, one of the following readings may be used at the discretion of the celebrant:

FROM THE OLD TESTAMENT

[Gather for me seventy men of the elders of Israel]

A Reading (Lesson) from the Book of Numbers [11:16-17]

The Lord said to Moses, "Gather for me seventy men of the elders of Israel, whom you know to be the elders of the people and officers over them; and bring them to the tent of meeting, and let them take their stand there with you. And I will come down and talk with you there; and I will take some of the spirit which is upon you and put it upon them; and they shall bear the burden of the people with you, that you may not bear it yourself alone."

or this

[Give heed to the statutes and ordinances which I teach you]

A Reading (Lesson) from the Book of Deuteronomy [4:1-2,9]

Moses said, "And now, O Israel, give heed to the statutes and the ordinances which I teach you, and do them; that you may live, and go in and take possession of the land which the Lord, the God of your fathers, gives you. You shall not add to the word which I command you, nor take from it; that you may keep the commandments of the Lord your God which I command you. Only take heed, and keep your soul diligently, lest you forget the things which your eyes have seen, and lest they depart from your heart all the days of your life; make them known to your children and your children's children."

or this

[Some of them had charge of the utensils of service]

A Reading (Lesson) from the First Book of the Chronicles [9:26-30,32]

The four chief gatekeepers, who were Levites, were in charge of the chambers and the treasures of the house of God. And they lodged round about the house of God; for upon them lay the duty of watching, and they had charge of opening it every morning. Some of them had charge of the utensils of service, for they were required to count them when they were brought in and taken out. Others of them were appointed over the furniture, and over all the holy utensils, also over the fine flour, the wine, the oil, the incense, and the spices. Others, of the sons of the priests, prepared the mixing of the spices. Also some of their kinsmen of the Ko'hathites had charge of the showbread, to prepare it every sabbath.

or the following

[Ezra reads the Law of Moses to the people]

A Reading (Lesson) from the Book of Nehemiah
[8:1-4a,5-6,8]

All the people gathered as one man into the square before the Water Gate; and they told Ezra the scribe to bring the book of the law of Moses which the Lord had given to Israel. And Ezra the priest brought the law before the assembly, both men and women and all who could hear with understanding, on the first day of the seventh month. And he read from it facing the square before the Water Gate from early morning until midday, in the presence of the men and women and those who could understand; and the ears of all the people were attentive to the book of the law. And Ezra the scribe stood on a wooden pulpit which they had made for the purpose. And Ezra opened the book in the sight of all the people, for he was above all the people; and when he opened it all the people stood. And Ezra blessed the Lord, the great God; and all the people answered, "Amen, Amen," lifting up their hands; and they bowed their heads and worshiped the Lord with their faces to the ground. And they read from the book, from the law of God, clearly; and they gave the sense, so that the people understood the reading.

or this

[Having gifts that differ according to the grace given]

A Reading (Lesson) from the Letter of Paul to the Romans [12:6-12]

Having gifts that differ according to the grace given to us, let us use them: if prophecy, in proportion to our faith; if service, in our serving; he who teaches, in his teaching; he who exhorts, in his exhortation; he who contributes, in liberality; he who gives aid, with zeal; he who does acts of mercy, with cheerfulness. Let love be genuine; hate what is evil, hold fast to what is good; love one another with brotherly affection; outdo one another in showing honor. Never flag in zeal, be aglow with the Spirit, serve the Lord. Rejoice in your hope, be patient in tribulation, be constant in prayer.

or this

[Having this ministry by the mercy of God]

A Reading (Lesson) from the Second Letter of Paul to the Corinthians [4:2,5-6]

We have renounced disgraceful, underhanded ways; we refuse to practice cunning or to tamper with God's word, but by the open statement of the truth we could commend ourselves to every man's conscience in the sight of God. For what we preach is not ourselves, but Jesus Christ as Lord, with ourselves as your servants for Jesus' sake. For it is the God who said, "Let light shine out of darkness," who has shone in our hearts to give the light of the glory of God in the face of Christ.

or the following

[Sing psalms and hymns and spiritual songs]

*A Reading (Lesson) from the Letter of Paul
to the Colossians* [3:12-17]

Put on then, as God's chosen ones, holy and beloved,
compassion, kindesss, lowliness, meekness, and patience,
forbearing one another and, if one has a complaint against
another, forgiving each other; as the Lord has forgiven
you, so you also must forgive. And above all these put on
love, which binds everything together in perfect harmony.
And let the peace of Christ rule in your hearts, to which
indeed you were called in the one body. And be thankful.
Let the word of Christ dwell in you richly, teach and
admonish one another in all wisdom, and sing psalms and
hymns and spiritual songs with thankfulness in your
hearts to God. And whatever you do, in word or deed, do
everything in the name of the Lord Jesus, giving thanks to
God the Father through him.

or this

[God is not so unjust as to overlook your work and love]

A Reading (Lesson) from the Letter to the Hebrews
[6:9-12]

Though we speak thus, yet in your case, beloved, we feel
sure of better things that belong to salvation. For God is
not so unjust as to overlook your work and the love which
you showed for his sake in serving the saints, as you still
do. And we desire each one of you to show the same
earnestness in realizing the full assurance of hope until the
end, so that you may not be sluggish, but imitators of
those who through faith and patience inherit the promises.

or this

[You are the light of the world]

*A Reading (Lesson) from the Gospel
According to Matthew* [5:14-16]

Jesus said, "You are the light of the world. A city set on a hill cannot be hid. Nor do men light a lamp and put it under a bushel, but on a stand, and it gives light to all in the house. Let your light so shine before men, that they may see your good works and give glory to your Father who is in heaven."

or this

[A sower went forth to sow]

*A Reading (Lesson) from the Gospel
According to Mark* [4:2-9]

Jesus taught them many things in parables, and in his teaching he said to them: "Listen! A sower went out to sow. And as he sowed, some seed fell along the path, and the birds came and devoured it. Other seed fell on rocky ground, where it had not much soil, and immediately it sprang up, since it had no depth of soil; and when the sun rose it was scorched, and since it had no root it withered away. Other seed fell among thorns and the thorns grew up and choked it, and it yielded no grain. And other seeds fell into good soil and brought forth grain, growing up and increasing and yielding thirtyfold and sixtyfold and a hundredfold." And he said, "He who has ears to hear, let him hear."

or the following

[He will come and serve them]

*A Reading (Lesson) from the Gospel
According to Luke* [12:35-37]

Jesus said to his disciples, "Let your loins be girded and your lamps burning, and be like men who are waiting for their master to come home from the marriage feast, so that they may open to him at once when he comes and knocks. Blessed are those servants whom the master finds awake when he comes; truly, I say to you, he will gird himself and have them sit at table, and he will come and serve them."

or this

[There is a lad here who has five barley loaves]

*A Reading (Lesson) from the Gospel
According to John* [6:(1-7)8-13]

Jesus went to the other side of the Sea of Galilee, which is the sea of Tibe'ri-as. And a multitude followed him, because they saw the signs which he did on those who were diseased. Jesus went up on the mountain, and there sat down with his disciples. Now the Passover, the feast of the Jews, was at hand. Lifting up his eyes, then, and seeing that a multitude was coming to him, Jesus said to Philip, "How are we to buy bread, so that these people may eat?" This he said to test him, for he himself knew what he would do. Philip answered him, "Two hundred denarii would not buy enough bread for each of them to get a little."

[Seeing that a multitude was coming to him, Jesus said to Philip, "How are we to buy bread, so that these people may eat?"]
One of the disciples, Andrew, Simon Peter's brother, said

to him, "There is a lad here who has five barley loaves and two fish; but what are they among so many?" Jesus said, "Make the people sit down." Now there was much grass in the place; so the men sat down, in number about five thousand. Jesus then took the loaves, and when he had given thanks, he distributed them to those who were seated; so also the fish, as much as they wanted. And when they had eaten their fill, he told his disciples, "Gather up the fragments left over, that nothing may be lost." So they gathered them up and filled twelve baskets with fragments from the five barley loaves, left by those who had eaten.

The Founding of a Church
[BOS, pages 198, 200]

Ground Breaking

A Reading (Lesson) from the Book of Genesis [28:10-17]

Jacob left Beer-sheba, and went toward Haran. And he came to a certain place, and stayed there that night, because the sun had set. Taking one of the stones of the place, he put it under his head and lay down in that place to sleep. And he dreamed that there was a ladder set up on the earth, and the top of it reached to heaven; and behold, the angels of God were ascending and descending on it! And behold, the Lord stood above it and said, "I am the Lord, the God of Abraham your father and the God of Isaac; the land on which you lie I will give to you and to your descendants; and your descendants shall be like the dust of the earth, and you shall spread abroad to the west and to the east and to the north and to the south; and by you and your descendants shall all the families of the earth bless themselves. Behold, I am with you and will keep you wherever you go, and will bring you back to this land; for I will not leave you until I have done that of which I have spoken to you." Then Jacob awoke from his sleep and said, "Surely the Lord is in this place; and I did not know it." And he was afraid, and said, "How awesome is this place! This is none other than the house of God, and this is the gate of heaven."

Laying of a Cornerstone

A Reading (Lesson) from the Letter of Paul to the Ephesians [2:19-22]

So then you are no longer strangers and sojourners, but you are fellow citizens with the saints and members of the household of God, built upon the foundation of the apostles and prophets, Christ Jesus himself being the cornerstone, in whom the whole structure is joined together and grows into a holy temple in the Lord; in whom you also are built into it for a dwelling place of God in the Spirit.

IV
Episcopal Services

Episcopal Services

A Proper for the Consecration of Chrism

[BOS, page 211]

If there is a need to consecrate Chrism at a separate, diocesan, service, the Proper Collect is on page 211 of BOS. The following Proper Readings may be used.

A Reading (Lesson) from the Book of Isaiah [61:1-8]

The Spirit of the Lord God is upon me, because the Lord has anointed me to bring good tidings to the afflicted; he has sent me to bind up the brokenhearted, to proclaim liberty to the captives, and the opening of the prison to those who are bound; to proclaim the year of the Lord's favor, and the day of vengeance of our God; to comfort all who mourn; to grant to those who mourn in Zion—to give them a garland instead of ashes, the oil of gladness instead of mourning, the mantle of praise instead of a faint spirit; that they may be called oaks of righteousness, the planting of the Lord, that he may be glorified. They shall build up the ancient ruins, they shall raise up the former devastations; they shall repair the ruined cities, the devastations of many generations. Aliens shall stand and feed your flocks, foreigners shall be your plowmen and vinedressers; but you shall be called the priests of the Lord, men shall speak of you as the ministers of our God;

you shall eat the wealth of the nations, and in their riches you shall glory. Instead of your shame you shall have a double portion, instead of dishonor you shall rejoice in your lot; therefore in your land you shall possess a double portion; yours shall be everlasting joy. For I the Lord love justice, I hate robbery and wrong; I will faithfully give them their recompense, and I will make an everlasting covenant with them.

Psalm 23 [page 612] or *Psalm 89:20-29* [page 715]

A Reading (Lesson) from the Revelation to John [1:4-8]

John to the seven churches that are in Asia: Grace to you and peace from him who is and who was and who is to come, and from the seven spirits who are before his throne, and from Jesus Christ the faithful witness, the first-born of the dead, and the ruler of kings on earth. To him who loves us and has freed us from our sins by his blood and made us a kingdom, priests to his God and Father, to him be glory and dominion for ever and ever. Amen. Behold, he is coming with the clouds, and every eye will see him, every one who pierced him; and all tribes of the earth will wail on account of him. Even so. Amen. "I am the Alpha and the Omega," says the Lord God, who is and who was and who is to come, the Almighty.

✠ *The Holy Gospel of Our Lord Jesus Christ According to Luke* [4:16-21]

Jesus came to Nazareth, where he had been brought up; and he went to the synagogue, as his custom was, on the sabbath day. And he stood up to read; and there was given to him the book of the prophet Isaiah. He opened the book and found the place where it was written, "The

Spirit of the Lord is upon me, because he has anointed me to preach good news to the poor. He has sent me to proclaim release to the captives and recovering of sight to the blind, to set at liberty those who are oppressed, to proclaim the acceptable year of the Lord." And he closed the book, and gave it back to the attendant, and sat down; and the eyes of all in the synagogue were fixed on him. And he began to say to them, "Today this scripture has been fulfilled in your hearing."

Ordination of a Bishop
[BCP, page 515]

Three Lessons are read. Lay persons read the Old Testament Lesson and the Epistle.

The Readings are ordinarily selected from the following list and may be lengthened if desired. On a Major Feast or on a Sunday, the Presiding Bishop may select Readings from the Proper of the Day.

FROM THE OLD TESTAMENT

Isaiah 61:1-8 [page 189 above]

or this

A Reading (Lesson) from the Book of Isaiah [42:1-9]

Behold my servant, whom I uphold, my chosen, in whom my soul delights; I have put my Spirit upon him, he will bring forth justice to the nations. He will not cry or lift up his voice, or make it heard in the street; a bruised reed he will not break, and a dimly burning wick he will not quench; he will faithfully bring forth justice. He will not fail or be discouraged till he has established justice in the earth; and the coastlands wait for his law. Thus says God, the Lord, who created the heavens and stretched them out, who spread forth the earth and what comes from it, who gives breath to the people upon it and the spirit to those who walk in it: "I am the Lord, I have called you in righteousness, I have taken you by the hand and kept you; I have given you as a covenant to the people, a light to the nations, to open the eyes that are blind, to bring out the prisoners from the dungeon, from the prison those who sit in darkness. I am the Lord, that is my name; my glory I give to no other, nor my praise to graven images. Behold the former things have come to pass, and new things I now declare; before they spring forth I tell you of them."

Psalm 99 [page 728]   or   *Psalm 40:1-14* [page 640]   or

Psalm 100 [page 729]

FROM THE NEW TESTAMENT

A Reading (Lesson) from the Letter to the Hebrews
[5:1-10]

Every high priest chosen from among men is appointed to act on behalf of men in relation to God, to offer gifts and sacrifices for sins. He can deal gently with the ignorant and wayward, since he himself is beset with weakness. Because of this he is bound to sacrifice for his own sins as well as for those of the people. And one does not take the honor upon himself, but he is called by God, just as Aaron was. So also Christ did not exalt himself to be made a high priest, but was appointed by him who said to him, "Thou art my Son, today I gave begotten thee"; as he says also in another place, "Thou art a priest for ever, after the order of Melchiz'edek." In the days of his flesh, Jesus offered up prayers and supplications, with loud cries and tears, to him who was able to save him from death, and he was heard for his godly fear. Although he was a Son, he learned obedience through what he suffered; and being made perfect he became the source of eternal salvation to all who obey him, being designated by God a high priest after the order of Melchiz'edek.

or this

A Reading (Lesson) from the First Letter of Paul to Timothy [3:1-7]

The saying is sure: If any one aspires to the office of bishop, he desires a noble task. Now a bishop must be above reproach, the husband of one wife, temperate, sensible, dignified, hospitable, an apt teacher, no drunkard, not violent but gentle, not quarrelsome, and no lover of money. He must manage his own household well, keeping his children submissive and respectful in every way; for if a man does not know how to manage his own household, how can he care for God's church? He must not be a recent convert, or he may be puffed up with conceit and fall into the condemnation of the devil; moreover he must be well thought of by outsiders, or he may fall into reproach and the snare of the devil.

or the following

*A Reading (Lesson) from the Second Letter of Paul
to the Corinthians* [3:4-9]

Such is the confidence that we have through Christ toward
God. Not that we are competent of ourselves to claim
anything as coming from us; our competence is from God,
who has made us competent to be ministers of a new
covenant, not in a written code but in the Spirit; for the
written code kills, but the Spirit gives life. Now if the
dispensation of death, carved in letters on stone, came
with such splendor that the Israelites could not look at
Moses' face because of its brightness, fading as this was,
will not the dispensation of the Spirit be attended with
greater splendor? For if there was splendor in the
dispensation of condemnation, the dispensation of
righteousness must far exceed it in splendor.

FROM THE HOLY GOSPEL

✝ *The Holy Gospel of Our Lord Jesus Christ
According to John* [20:19-23]

On the evening of the first day of the week, the doors
being shut where the disciples were, for fear of the Jews,
Jesus came and stood among them and said to them,
"Peace be with you." When he said this, he showed them
his hands and his side. Then the disciples were glad when
they saw the Lord. Jesus said to them again, "Peace be
with you. As the Father has sent me, even so I send you."
And when he had said this, he breathed on them, and said
to them, "Receive the Holy Spirit. If you forgive the sins
of any, they are forgiven; if you retain the sins of any, they
are retained."

or this

✝ *The Holy Gospel of Our Lord Jesus Christ*
According to John [17:1-9,18-21]

Jesus lifted up his eyes to heaven and said, "Father, the hour has come; glorify thy Son that the Son may glorify thee, since thou hast given him power over all flesh, to give eternal life to all whom thou hast given him. And this is eternal life, that they know thee the only true God, and Jesus Christ whom thou hast sent. I glorified thee on earth, having accomplished the work which thou gavest me to do; and now, Father, glorify thou me in thy own presence with the glory which I had with thee before the world was made. I have manifested thy name to the men whom thou gavest me out of the world; thine they were, and thou gavest them to me, and they have kept thy word. Now they know that everything that thou hast given me is from thee; for I have given them the words which thou gavest me, and they have received them and know in truth that I came from thee; and they have believed that thou didst send me. I am praying for them; I am not praying for the world but for those whom thou hast given me, for they are thine. As thou didst send me into the world, so I have sent them into the world. And for their sake I consecrate myself, that they also may be consecrated in truth. I do not pray for these only, but also for those who believe in me through their word, that they may all be one; even as thou, Father, art in me, and I in thee, that they also may be in us, so that the world may believe that thou hast sent me."

or this

✝ *The Holy Gospel of Our Lord Jesus Christ*
According to Luke [24:44-49a]

Jesus said to the disciples, "These are my words which I spoke to you, while I was still with you, that everything written about me in the law of Moses and the prophets and the psalms must be fulfilled." Then he opened their minds to understand the scriptures, and said to them, "Thus it is written, that the Christ should suffer and on the third day rise from the dead, and that repentance and forgiveness of sins should be preached in his name to all nations, beginning from Jerusalem. You are witnesses of these things. And behold, I send the promise of my Father upon you."

Ordination of a Priest

[BCP, page 528]

The Readings are ordinarily selected from the following list and may be lengthened if desired. On a Major Feast, or on a Sunday, the Bishop may select Readings from the Proper of the Day.

FROM THE OLD TESTAMENT

A Reading (Lesson) from the Book of Isaiah [6:1-8]

In the year that King Uzzi'ah died I saw the Lord sitting upon a throne, high and lifted up; and his train filled the temple. Above him stood the seraphim; each had six wings: with two he covered his face, and with two he covered his feet, and with two he flew. And one called to another and said: "Holy, holy, holy is the Lord of hosts; the whole earth is full of his glory." And the foundations of the thresholds shook at the voice of him who called, and the house was filled with smoke. And I said: "Woe is me! For I am lost; for I am a man of unclean lips, and I dwell in the midst of a people of unclean lips; for my eyes have seen the King, the Lord of hosts!" Then flew one of the seraphim to me, having in his hand a burning coal which he had taken with tongs from the altar. And he touched my mouth, and said: "Behold, this has touched your lips; your guilt is taken away, and your sin forgiven." And I heard the voice of the Lord saying, "Whom shall I send, and who will go for us?" Then I said, "Here am I! Send me."

or this

A Reading (Lesson) from the Book of Numbers
[11:16-17,24-25 (omitting the final clause)]

The Lord said to Moses, "Gather for me seventy men of the elders of Israel, whom you know to be the elders of the people and officers over them; and bring them to the tent of meeting, and let them take their stand there with you. And I will come down and talk with you there; and I will take some of the spirit which is upon you and put it upon them; and they shall bear the burden of the people with you, that you may not bear it yourself alone." So Moses went out and told the people the words of the Lord; and he gathered seventy men of the elders of the people, and placed them round about the tent. Then the Lord came down in the cloud and spoke to him, and took some of the spirit that was upon him and put it upon the seventy elders; and when the spirit rested upon them, they prophesied.

Psalm 43 [page 644] or *Psalm 132:8-19* [page 786]

A Reading (Lesson) from the First Letter of Peter [5:1-4]*

I exhort the presbyters among you, as a fellow presbyter and a witness of the sufferings of Christ as well as a partaker in the glory that is to be revealed. Tend the flock of God that is your charge, not by constraint but willingly, not for shameful gain but eagerly, not as domineering over those in your charge but being examples to the flock. And when the chief Shepherd is manifested you will obtain the unfading crown of glory.

or this

A Reading (Lesson) from the Letter of Paul to the Ephesians [4:7,11-16]

Grace was given to each of us according to the measure of Christ's gift. And his gifts were that some should be apostles, some prophets, some evangelists, some pastors and teachers, to equip the saints for the work of ministry, for building up the body of Christ, until we all attain to the unity of the faith and of the knowledge of the Son of God, to mature manhood, to the measure of the stature of the fulness of Christ; so that we may no longer be children, tossed to and fro and carried about with every wind of doctrine, by the cunning of men, by their craftiness in deceitful wiles. Rather, speaking the truth in love, we are to grow up in every way into him who is the head, into Christ, from whom the whole body, joined and

---

*It is to be noted that where the words elder, elders, and fellow elder, appear in translations of 1 Peter 5:1, the original Greek terms presbyter, presbyters, and fellow presbyter, are to be substituted.

knit together by every joint with which it is supplied, when each part is working properly, makes bodily growth and upbuilds itself in love.

or this

A Reading (Lesson) from the Letter of Paul to the Philippians [4:4-9]

Rejoice in the Lord always; again I will say, Rejoice. Let all men know your forbearance. The Lord is at hand. Have no anxiety about anything, but in everything by prayer and supplication with thanksgiving let your requests be made known to God. And the peace of God, which passes all understanding, will keep your hearts and your minds in Christ Jesus. Finally, brethren, whatever is true, whatever is honorable, whatever is just, whatever is pure, whatever is lovely, whatever is gracious, if there is any excellence, if there is anything worthy of praise, think about these things. What you have learned and received and heard and seen in me, do; and the God of peace will be with you.

FROM THE HOLY GOSPEL

✝ *The Holy Gospel of Our Lord Jesus Christ According to Matthew* [9:35-38]

Jesus went about all the cities and villages, teaching in their synagogues and preaching the gospel of the kingdom, and healing every disease and every infirmity. When he saw the crowds, he had compassion for them, because they were harassed and helpless, like sheep without a shepherd. Then he said to his disciples, "The harvest is plentiful, but the laborers are few; pray therefore the Lord of the harvest to send out laborers into his harvest."

or this

✠ *The Holy Gospel of Our Lord Jesus Christ According to John* [10:11-18]

Jesus said, "I am the good shepherd. The good shepherd lays down his life for the sheep. He who is a hireling and not a shepherd, whose own the sheep are not, sees the wolf coming and leaves the sheep and flees; and the wolf snatches them and scatters them. He flees because he is a hireling and cares nothing for the sheep. I am the good shepherd; I know my own and my own know me, as the Father knows me and I know the Father; and I lay down my life for the sheep. And I have other sheep, that are not of this fold; I must bring them also, and they will heed my voice. So there shall be one flock, one shepherd. For this reason the Father loves me, because I lay down my life, that I may take it again. No one takes it from me, but I lay it down of my own accord. I have power to lay it down, and I have power to take it again; this charge I have received from my Father."

or this

✠ *The Holy Gospel of Our Lord Jesus Christ According to John* [6:35-38]

Jesus said to the people, "I am the bread of life; he who comes to me shall not hunger, and he who believes in me shall never thirst. But I said to you that you have seen me and yet do not believe. All that the Father gives me will come to me; and him who comes to me I will not cast out. For I have come down from heaven, not to do my own will, but the will of him who sent me."

Ordination of a Deacon

[BCP, page 540]

The Readings are ordinarily selected from the following list and may be lengthened if desired. On a Major Feast, or on a Sunday, the Bishop may select Readings from the Proper of the Day.

FROM THE OLD TESTAMENT

A Reading (Lesson) from the Book of Jeremiah [1:4-9]

The word of the Lord came to me saying, "Before I formed you in the womb I knew you, and before you were born I consecrated you; I appointed you a prophet to the nations." Then I said, "Ah, Lord God! Behold, I do not know how to speak, for I am only a youth." But the Lord said to me, "Do not say, 'I am a youth'; for to all whom I send you you shall go, and whatever I command you you shall speak. Be not afraid of them, for I am with you to deliver you, says the Lord." Then the Lord put forth his hand and touched my mouth; and the Lord said to me, "Behold, I have put my words in your mouth."

or this

A Reading (Lesson) from the Book of Ecclesiasticus [39:1-8]

He who devotes himself to the study of the law of the Most High will seek out the wisdom of all the ancients, and will be concerned with prophecies; he will preserve the discourse of notable men and penetrate the subtleties of parables; he will seek out the hidden meanings of proverbs and be at home with the obscurities of parables.

He will serve among great men and appear before rulers; he will travel through the lands of foreign nations, for he tests the good and the evil among men. He will set his heart to rise early to seek the Lord who made him, and will make supplication before the Most High; he will open his mouth in prayer and make supplication for his sins. If the great Lord is willing, he will be filled with the spirit of understanding; he will put forth words of wisdom and give thanks to the Lord in prayer. He will direct his counsel and knowledge aright, and meditate on his secrets. He will reveal instruction in his teaching, and will glory in the law of the Lord's covenant.

Psalm 84 [page 707]   or   *Psalm 119:33-40* [page 766]

FROM THE NEW TESTAMENT

A Reading (Lesson) from the Second Letter of Paul to the Corinthians [4:1-6]

Having this ministry by the mercy of God, we do not lose heart. We have renounced disgraceful, underhanded ways; we refuse to practice cunning or to tamper with God's word, but by the open statement of the truth we would commend ourselves to every man's conscience in the sight of God. And even if our gospel is veiled, it is veiled only to those who are perishing. In their case the god of this world has blinded the minds of the unbelievers, to keep them from seeing the light of the gospel of the glory of Christ, who is the likeness of God. For what we preach is not ourselves, but Jesus Christ as Lord, with ourselves as your servants for Jesus' sake. For it is the God who said, "Let light shine out of darkness," who has shone in our hearts to give the light of the knowledge of the glory of God in the face of Christ.

or this

A Reading (Lesson) from the First Letter of Paul to Timothy [3:8-13]

Deacons must be serious, not double-tongued, not addicted to much wine, not greedy for gain; they must hold the mystery of the faith with a clear conscience. And let them also be tested first; then if they prove themselves blameless let them serve as deacons. The women likewise must be serious, no slanderers, but temperate, faithful in all things. Let deacons be the husband of one wife, and let them manage their children and their households well; for those who serve well as deacons gain a good standing for themselves and also great confidence in the faith which is in Christ Jesus.

or this

A Reading (Lesson) from the Acts of the Apostles [6:2-7]

The twelve summoned the body of the disciples and said, "It is not right that we should give up preaching the word of God to serve tables. Therefore, brethren, pick out from among you seven men of good repute, full of the Spirit and of wisdom, whom we may appoint to this duty. But we will devote ourselves to prayer and to the ministry of the word." And what they said pleased the whole multitude, and they chose Stephen, a man full of faith and of the Holy Spirit, and Philip, and Proch'orus, and Nica'nor, and Timon, and Par'menas, and Nicola'us, a proselyte of Antioch. These they set before the apostles, and they prayed and laid their hands upon them. And the word of God increased; and the number of the disciples multiplied greatly in Jerusalem, and a great many of the priests were obedient to the faith.

FROM THE HOLY GOSPEL

✝ *The Holy Gospel of Our Lord Jesus Christ According to Luke* [12:35-38]

Jesus said to his disciples, "Let your loins be girded and your lamps burning, and be like men who are waiting for their master to come home from the marriage feast, so that they may open to him at once when he comes and knocks. Blessed are those servants, whom the master finds awake when he comes; truly, I say to you, he will gird himself and have them sit at table, and he will come and serve them. If he comes in the second watch, or in the third, and finds them so, blessed are those servants!"

or this

✝ *The Holy Gospel of Our Lord Jesus Christ According to Luke* [22:24-27]

A dispute arose among the apostles which of them was to be regarded as the greatest. And Jesus said to them, "The kings of the Gentiles exercise lordship over them; and those in authority over them are called benefactors. But not so with you; rather let the greatest among you become as the youngest, and the leader as one who serves. For which is the greater, one who sits at table, or one who serves? Is it not the one who sits at table? But I am among you as one who serves."

Celebration of a New Ministry

[BCP, page 560]

The Readings are selected from the following list, or from the Proper of the Day. Other passages suitable to the circumstances may be substituted. Appropriate selections may be found in the Service for the Ordination of a Deacon (page 201 above) or in the Lectionary for Various Occasions (pages 227-275 below).

FROM THE OLD TESTAMENT

A Reading (Lesson) from the Book of Joshua [1:7-9]

The Lord said to Joshua the son of Nun, Moses' minister, "Only be strong and very courageous, being careful to do according to all the law which Moses my servant commanded you; turn not from it to the right hand or to the left, that you may have good success wherever you go. This book of the law shall not depart out of your mouth, but you shall meditate on it day and night, that you may be careful to do according to all that is written in it; for then you shall make your way prosperous, and then you shall have good success. Have I not commanded you? Be strong and of good courage; be not frightened, neither be dismayed; for the Lord your God is with you wherever you go."

or this

A Reading (Lesson) from the Book of Numbers [11:16-17,24-25a]

The Lord said to Moses, "Gather for me seventy men of the elders of Israel, whom you know to be the elders of the people and officers over them; and bring them to the tent of meeting, and let them take their stand there with you. And I will come down and talk with you there; and I will take some of the spirit which is upon you and put it upon them; and they shall bear the burden of the people with you, that you may not bear it yourself alone." So Moses went out and told the people the words of the Lord; and he gathered seventy men of the elders of the people, and placed them round about the tent. Then the Lord came down in the cloud and spoke to him, and took some of the spirit that was upon him and put it upon the seventy elders.

Psalm 43 [page 644]   or   *Psalm 132:1-9* [page 785]   or

Psalm 146 [page 803]   or

Psalms 133 & 134 (especially suitable for use in the evening) [page 787]

FROM THE NEW TESTAMENT

A Reading (Lesson) from the Letter of Paul to the Romans [12:1-18]

I appeal to you therefore, brethren, by the mercies of God, to present your bodies as a living sacrifice, holy and acceptable to God, which is your spiritual worship. Do not be conformed to this world but be transformed by the renewal of your mind, that you may prove what is the will of God, what is good and acceptable and perfect. For by the grace given to me I bid every one among you not to think of himself more highly than he ought to think, but to think with sober judgment, each according to the measure of faith which God has assigned him. For as in one body we have many members, and all the members do not have the same function, so we, though many, are one body in Christ, and individually members one of another. Having gifts that differ according to the grace given to us, let us use them: if prophecy, in proportion to our faith; if service, in our serving; he who teaches, in his teaching; he who exhorts, in his exhortation; he who contributes, in liberality; he who gives aid, with zeal; he who does acts of mercy, with cheerfulness. Let love be genuine; hate what is evil, hold fast to what is good; love one another with brotherly affection; outdo one another in showing honor. Never flag in zeal, be aglow with the Spirit, serve the Lord. Rejoice in your hope, be patient in tribulation, be constant in prayer. Contribute to the needs of the saints, practice hospitality. Bless those who persecute you; bless and do not curse them. Rejoice with those who rejoice, weep with those who weep. Live in harmony with one another; do not be haughty, but associate with the lowly; never be conceited. Repay no one evil for evil, but take thought for what is noble in the sight of all. If possible, so far as it depends upon you, live peaceably with all.

or this

A Reading (Lesson) from the Letter of Paul to the Ephesians [4:7,11-16]

Grace was given to each of us according to the measure of Christ's gift. And his gifts were that some should be apostles, some prophets, some evangelists, some pastors and teachers, to equip the saints for the work of ministry, for building up the body of Christ, until we all attain to the unity of the faith and of the knowledge of the Son of God, to mature manhood, to the measure of the stature of the fulness of Christ; so that we may no longer be children, tossed to and fro and carried about with every wind of doctrine, by the cunning of men, by their craftiness in deceitful wiles. Rather, speaking the truth in love, we are to grow up in every way into him who is the head, into Christ, from whom the whole body, joined and knit together by every joint with which it is supplied, when each part is working properly, makes bodily growth and upbuilds itself in love.

FROM THE HOLY GOSPEL

✝ *The Holy Gospel of Our Lord Jesus Christ According to John* [15:9-16]

Jesus said to his disciples, "As the Father has loved me, so have I loved you; abide in my love. If you keep my commandments, you will abide in my love, just as I have kept my Father's commandments and abide in his love. These things I have spoken to you, that my joy may be in you, and that your joy may be full. This is my commandment, that you love one another as I have loved you. Greater love has no man than this, that a man lay down his life for his friends. You are my friends if you do what I command you. No longer do I call you servants, for the servant does not know what his master is doing; but I have called you my friends, for all that I have heard from my Father I have made known to you. You did not choose me, but I chose you and appointed you that you should go and bear fruit and that your fruit should abide; so that whatever you ask the Father in my name, he may give it to you."

or this

✝ *The Holy Gospel of Our Lord Jesus Christ*
According to Luke [10:1-2]

After this the Lord appointed seventy others, and sent them on ahead of him, two by two, into every town and place where he himself was about to come. And he said to them, "The harvest is plentiful, but the laborers are few; pray therefore the Lord of the harvest to send out laborers into his harvest."

or this

✝ *The Holy Gospel of Our Lord Jesus Christ*
According to John [14:11-15]

Jesus said to Philip, "Believe me that I am in the Father and the Father in me; or else believe me for the sake of the works themselves. Truly, truly, I say to you, he who believes in me will also do the works that I do; and greater works than these will he do, because I go to the Father. Whatever you ask in my name, I will do it, that the Father may be glorified in the Son; if you ask anything in my name, I will do it. If you love me, you will keep my commandments."

The Dedication and Consecration of a Church

[BCP, page 571]

Three Lessons are read. Lay persons read the Old Testament Lesson and the Epistle. Selections are ordinarily made from among the following, but on a Major Feast, Sunday, or Patronal Feast, selections may be made from the Proper of the Day.

FROM THE OLD TESTAMENT

A Reading (Lesson) from the First Book of the Kings
[8:22-23,27b-30]

Solomon stood before the altar of the Lord in the presence of all the assembly of Israel, and spread forth his hands toward heaven; and said, "O Lord, God of Israel, there is no God like thee, in heaven above or on earth beneath, keeping covenant and showing steadfast love to thy servants who walk before thee with all their heart. Behold, heaven and the highest heaven cannot contain thee; how much less this house which I have built! Yet have regard to the prayer of thy servant and to his supplication, O Lord my God, hearkening to the cry and to the prayer which thy servant prays before thee this day; that thy eyes may be open night and day toward this house, the place of which thou hast said, 'My name shall be there,' that thou mayest hearken to the prayer which thy servant offers toward this place. And hearken thou to the supplication of they servant and of thy people Israel, when they pray toward this place; yea, hear thou in heaven thy dwelling place; and when thou hearest, forgive."

or this

A Reading (Lesson) from the Second Book of Samuel
[6:12-15,17-19]

It was told King David, "The Lord has blessed the household of O'bed-e'dom and all that belongs to him, because of the ark of God." So David went and brought up the ark of God from the house of O'bed-e'dom to the city of David with rejoicing; and when those who bore the ark of the Lord had gone six paces, he sacrificed an ox and a fatling. And David danced before the Lord with all his might; and David was girded with a linen ephod. So David and all the houses of Israel brought up the ark of the Lord with shouting and with the sound of the horn. And they brought in the ark of the Lord, and set it in its place, inside the tent which David had pitched for it; and David offered burnt offerings and peace offerings before the Lord. And when David had finished offering the burnt offerings and the peace offerings, he blessed the people in the name of the Lord of hosts, and distributed among all the people, the whole multitude of Israel, both men and women, to each a cake of bread, a portion of meat, and a cake of raisins. Then all the people departed, each to his house.

Psalm 84 [page 707]   or   *Psalm 48* [page 651]

FROM THE NEW TESTAMENT

A Reading (Lesson) from the Revelation to John
[21:2-7]

I saw the holy city, new Jerusalem, coming down out of heaven from God, prepared as a bride adorned for her husband; and I heard a loud voice from the throne saying,

"Behold, the dwelling of God is with men. He will dwell with them, and they shall be his people, and God himself will be with them; he will wipe away every tear from their eyes, and death shall be no more, neither shall there be mourning nor crying nor pain any more, for the former things have passed away." And he who sat upon the throne said, "Behold, I make all things new." Also he said, "Write this, for these words are trustworthy and true." And he said to me, "It is done! I am the Alpha and the Omega, the beginning and the end. To the thirsty I will give from the fountain of the water of life without payment. He who conquers shall have this heritage, and I will be his God and he shall be my son."

or this

A Reading (Lesson) from the First Letter of Paul to the Corinthians [3:1-11,16-17]

I, brethren, could not address you as spiritual men, but as men of the flesh, as babes in Christ. I fed you with milk, not solid food; for you were not ready for it; and even yet you are not ready, for you are still of the flesh. For while there is jealousy and strife among you, are you not of the flesh, and behaving like ordinary men? For when one says, "I belong to Paul," and another, "I belong to Apol'los," are you not merely men? What then is Apol'los? What is Paul? Servants through whom you believed, as the Lord assigned to each. I planted, Apol'los watered, but God gave the growth. So neither he who plants nor he who waters is anything, but only God who gives the growth. He who plants and he who waters are equal, and each shall receive his wages according to his labor. For we are God's fellow workers; you are God's field, God's building. According to the grace of God given to me, like a skilled master builder I laid a foundation, and another man is building upon it. Let each man take care how he builds upon it. For no other foundation can any one lay than that which is laid, which is Jesus Christ. Do you not know that you are God's temple and that God's Spirit dwells in you? If any one destroys God's temple, God will destroy him. For God's temple is holy, and that temple you are.

or this

A Reading (Lesson) from the First Letter of Peter [2:1-9]

Put away all malice and all guile and insincerity and envy and all slander. Like newborn babes, long for the pure spiritual milk, that by it you may grow up to salvation: for you have tasted the kindness of the Lord. Come to him, to that living stone, rejected by men but in God's sight chosen and precious; and like living stones be yourselves built into a spiritual house, to be a holy priesthood, to offer spiritual sacrifices acceptable to God through Jesus Christ. For it stands in scripture: "Behold, I am laying in Zion a stone, a cornerstone chosen and precious, and he who believes in him will not be put to shame." To you therefore who believe, he is precious, but for those who do not believe, "The very stone which the builders rejected has become the head of the corner," and "A stone that will make men stumble, a rock that will make them fall"; for they stumble because they disobey the word, as they were destined to do. But you are a chosen race, a royal priesthood, a holy nation, God's own people, that you may declare the wonderful deeds of him who called you out of darkness into his marvelous light.

FROM THE HOLY GOSPEL

✝ *The Holy Gospel of Our Lord Jesus Christ According to Matthew* [7:13-14,24-25]

Jesus said to his disciples, "Enter by the narrow gate; for the gate is wide and the way is easy, that leads to destruction, and those who enter by it are many. For the gate is narrow and the way is hard, that leads to life, and those who find it are few. Every one then who hears these words of mine and does them will be like a wise man, who built his house upon the rock; and the rain fell, and the floods came, and the winds blew and beat upon that house, but it did not fall, because it had been founded on the rock."

or this

✝ *The Holy Gospel of Our Lord Jesus Christ According to Matthew* [21:10-14]

When Jesus entered Jerusalem, all the city was stirred, saying, "Who is this?" And the crowds said, "This is the prophet Jesus from Nazareth of Galilee." And Jesus entered the temple of God and drove out all who sold and bought in the temple, and he overturned the tables of the moneychangers and the seats of those who sold pigeons. He said to them, "It is written, 'My house shall be called a house of prayer'; but you make it a den of robbers." And the blind and the lame came to him in the temple, and he healed them.

Setting Apart for a Special Vocation

[BOS, page 229]

FROM THE OLD TESTAMENT

[The call of Abraham]

A Reading (Lesson) from the Book of Genesis
[12:1-4a(4b-8)]

The Lord said to Abram, "Go from your country and your kindred and your father's house to the land that I will show you. And I will make of you a great nation, and I will bless you, and make your name great, so that you will be a blessing. I will bless those who bless you, and him who curses you I will curse; and by you all the families of the earth shall bless themselves." So Abram went, as the Lord had told him.

and Lot went with him. Abram was seventy-five years old when he departed from Haran. And Abram took Sar'ai his wife, and Lot his brother's son, and all their possessions which they had gathered, and the persons that they had gotten in Haran; and they set forth to go to the land of Canaan. When they had come to the land of Canaan, Abram passed through the land to the place at Shechem, to the oak of Moreh. At that time the Canaanites were in the land. Then the Lord appeared to Abram, and said, "To your descendants I will give this land." So he built there an altar to the Lord, who had appeared to him. Thence he removed to the mountain on the east of Bethel, and pitched his tent, with Bethel on the west and Ai on the east; and there he built an altar to the Lord, and called on the name of the Lord.

or this

[The call of Samuel]

A Reading (Lesson) from the First Book of Samuel [3:1-11]

The boy Samuel was ministering to the Lord under Eli. And the word of the Lord was rare in those days; there was no frequent vision. At that time Eli, whose eyesight had begun to grow dim, so that he could not see, was lying down in his own place; the lamp of God had not yet gone out, and Samuel was lying down within the temple of the Lord, where the ark of God was. Then the Lord called, "Samuel! Samuel!" and he said, "Here I am!" and ran to Eli, and said, "Here I am, for you called me." But he said, "I did not call; lie down again." So he went and lay down. And the Lord called again, "Samuel!" And Samuel arose and went to Eli, and said, "Here I am, for you called me." But he said, "I did not call, my son; lie down again." Now Samuel did not yet know the Lord, and the word of the Lord had not yet been revealed to him. And the Lord called Samuel again the third time. And he arose and went to Eli, and said, "Here I am, for you called me." Then Eli perceived that the Lord was calling the boy. Therefore Eli said to Samuel, "Go, lie down; and if he calls you, you shall say, 'Speak, Lord, for thy servant hears.' " So Samuel went and lay down in his place. And the Lord came and stood forth, calling as at other times, "Samuel! Samuel!" And Samuel said, "Speak, for thy servant hears." Then the

Lord said to Samuel, "Behold, I am about to do a thing in Israel, at which the two ears of every one that hears it will tingle."

or this

[The call of Eli'sha]

A Reading (Lesson) from the First Book of the Kings [19:16b,19-21]

The Lord said to Eli'jah, "Eli'sha the son of Shaphat of A'bel-meho'lah you shall anoint to be prophet in your place." So he departed from there, and found Eli'sha the son of Shaphat, who was plowing, with twelve yoke of oxen before him, and he was with the twelfth. Eli'jah passed by him and cast his mantle upon him. And he left the oxen, and ran after Eli'jah, and said, "Let me kiss my father and my mother, and then I will follow you." And he said to him, "Go back again; for what have I done to you?" And he returned from following him, and took the yoke of oxen, and slew them, and boiled their flesh with the yokes of the oxen, and gave it to the people, and they ate. Then he arose and went after Eli'jah, and ministered to him.

Psalm 23 [page 612] or

Psalm 24:1-6(7-10) [page 613] or

Psalm 27:1-11(12-18) [page 617] or

Psalm 33:(1-11)12-22 [page 626] or

Psalm 34:1-8(9-22) [page 627] or

Psalm 40:1-12 [page 640] or

Psalm 63:1-12 [page 670] or *Psalm 100* [page 729]

[The apostles' teaching and fellowship]

A Reading (Lesson) from the Acts of the Apostles [2:42-47]

Those who were baptized devoted themselves to the apostles' teaching and fellowship, to the breaking of bread and the prayers. And fear came upon every soul; and many wonders and signs were done through the apostles. And all who believed were together and had all things in common; and they sold their possessions and goods and distributed them to all, as any had need. And day by day, attending the temple together and breaking bread in their homes, they partook of food with glad and generous hearts, praising God and having favor with all the people. And the Lord added to their number day by day those who were being saved.

or this

[They had everything in common]

A Reading (Lesson) from the Acts of the Apostles [4:32-35]

The company of those who believed were of one heart and soul, and no one said that any of the things which he possessed was his own, but they had everything in common. And with great power the apostles gave their testimony to the resurrection of the Lord Jesus, and great grace was upon them all. There was not a needy person among them, for as many as were possessors of lands or houses sold them, and brought the proceeds of what was sold and laid it at the apostles' feet; and distribution was made to each as any had need.

or this

[God chose what was foolish]

A Reading (Lesson) from the First Letter of Paul to the Corinthians [1:22-31]

Jews demand signs and Greeks seek wisdom, but we preach Christ crucified, a stumbling block to Jews and folly to Gentiles, but to those who are called, both Jews and Greeks, Christ the power of God and the wisdom of God. For the foolishness of God is wiser than men, and the weakness of God is stronger than men. For consider your call, brethren; not many of you were wise according to worldly standards, not many were powerful, not many were of noble birth; but God chose what is foolish in the world to shame the wise, God chose what is weak in the world to shame the strong, God chose what is low and despised in the world, even things that are not, to bring to nothing things that are, so that no human being might boast in the presence of God. He is the source of your life in Christ Jesus, whom God made our wisdom, our righteousness and sanctification and redemption; therefore, as it is written, "Let him who boasts, boast of the Lord."

or this

[That I may gain Christ]

A Reading (Lesson) from the Letter of Paul to the Philippians [3:8-14]

I count everything as loss because of the surpassing worth of knowing Christ Jesus my Lord. For his sake I have suffered the loss of all things, and count them as refuse, in order that I may gain Christ and be found in him, not having a righteousness of my own, based on law, but that which is through faith in Christ, the righteousness from God that depends on faith; that I may know him and the power of his resurrection, and may share his sufferings, becoming like him in his death, that if possible I may attain the resurrection from the dead. Not that I have already obtained this or am already perfect; but I press on to make it my own, because Christ Jesus has made me his own. Brethren, I do not consider that I have made it my own; but one thing I do, forgetting what lies behind and straining forward to what lies ahead, I press on toward the goal for the prize of the upward call of God in Christ Jesus.

or this

[Put on love, which binds everything together]

A Reading (Lesson) from the Letter of Paul to the Colossians [3:12-17]

Put on then, as God's chosen ones, holy and beloved, compassion, kindness, lowliness, meekness, and patience, forbearing one another and, if one has a complaint against another, forgiving each other; as the Lord has forgiven you, so you also must forgive. And above all these put on love, which binds everything together in perfect harmony. And let the peace of Christ rule in your hearts, to which indeed you were called in the one body. And be thankful. Let the word of Christ dwell in you richly, teach and admonish one another in all wisdom, and sing psalms and hymns and spiritual songs with thankfulness in your hearts to God. And whatever you do, in word or deed, do everything in the name of the Lord Jesus, giving thanks to God the Father through him.

or this

[He who abides in love abides in God]

A Reading (Lesson) from the First Letter of John [4:7-16]

Beloved, let us love one another; for love is of God, and he who loves is born of God and knows God. He who does not love does not know God; for God is love. In this the love of God was made manifest among us, that God sent his only Son into the world, so that we might live through him. In this is love, not that we loved God but that he loved us and sent his Son to be the expiation for our sins. Beloved, if God so loved us, we also ought to love one another. No man has ever seen God; if we love one another, God abides in us and his love is perfected in us. By this we know that we abide in him and he in us, because he has given us of his own Spirit. And we have seen and testify that the Father has sent his Son as the Savior of the world. Whoever confesses that Jesus is the Son of God, God abides in him, and he in God. So we know and believe the love God has for us. God is love, and he who abides in love abides in God, and God abides in him.

FROM THE HOLY GOSPEL

[Let him take up his cross and follow me]

✝ *The Holy Gospel of Our Lord Jesus Christ According to Matthew* [16:24-27]

Jesus told his disciples, "If any man would come after me, let him deny himself and take up his cross and follow me. For whoever would save his life will lose it, and whoever loses his life for my sake will find it. For what will it profit a man, if he gains the whole world and forfeits his life? Or what shall a man give in return for his life? For the Son of man is to come with his angels in the glory of his Father, and then he will repay every man for what he has done."

or this

[Eunuchs for the sake of the kingdom]

✝ *The Holy Gospel of Our Lord Jesus Christ According to Matthew* [19:3-12]

The Pharisees came up to Jesus and tested him by asking, "Is it lawful to divorce one's wife for any cause?" He answered, "Have you not read that he who made them from the beginning made them male and female, and said, 'For this reason a man shall leave his father and mother and be joined to his wife, and the two shall become one flesh'? So they are no longer two but one flesh. What therefore God has joined together, let not man put asunder." They said to him, "Why then did Moses command one to give a certificate of divorce, and to put her away?" He said to them, "For your hardness of heart Moses allowed you to divorce your wives, but from the beginning it was not so. And I say to you: whoever divorces his wife, except for unchastity, and marries another, commits adultery." The disciples said to him, "If such is the case of a man with his wife, it is not expedient to marry." But he said to them, "Not all men can receive this saying, but only those to whom it is given. For there are eunuchs who have been so from birth, and there are eunuchs who have been made eunuchs by men, and there are eunuchs who have made themselves eunuchs for the sake of the kingdom of heaven. He who is able to receive this, let him receive it."

or this

[Sell what you possess and give to the poor]

✝ *The Holy Gospel of Our Lord Jesus Christ*
According to Matthew [19:16-26]

A young man came up to Jesus, saying, "Teacher, what good deed must I do, to have eternal life?" And he said to him, "Why do you ask me about what is good? One there is who is good. If you would enter life, keep the commandments." He said to him, "Which?" And Jesus said, "You shall not kill, You shall not commit adultery, You shall not steal, You shall not bear false witness, Honor your father and mother, and, You shall love your neighbor as yourself." The young man said to him, "All these I have observed; what do I still lack?" Jesus said to him, "If you would be perfect, go, sell what you possess and give to the poor, and you will have treasure in heaven; and come, follow me." When the young man heard this he went away sorrowful; for he had great possessions. And Jesus said to his disciples, "Truly, I say to you, it will be hard for a rich man to enter the kingdom of heaven. Again I tell you, it is easier for a camel to go through the eye of a needle than for a rich man to enter the kingdom of God." When the disciples heard this they were greatly astonished, saying, "Who then can be saved?" But Jesus looked at them and said to them, "With men this is impossible, but with God all things are possible."

or the following

[I am the vine, you are the branches]

✝ *The Holy Gospel of Our Lord Jesus Christ According to John* [15:1-8]

Jesus said, "I am the true vine, and my Father is the vinedresser. Every branch of mine that bears no fruit, he takes away, and every branch that does bear fruit he prunes, that it may bear more fruit. You are already made clean by the word which I have spoken to you. Abide in me, and I in you. As the branch cannot bear fruit by itself, unless it abides in the vine, neither can you, unless you abide in me. I am the vine, you are the branches. He who abides in me, and I in him, he it is that bears much fruit, for apart from me you can do nothing. If a man does not abide in me, he is cast forth as a branch and withers; and the branches are gathered, thrown into the fire and burned. If you abide in me, and my words abide in you, ask whatever you will, and it shall be done for you. By this my Father is glorified, that you bear much fruit, and so prove to be my disciples."

V
Propers for Various Occasions

Propers for Various Occasions

[BCP, page 927]

1. Of the Holy Trinity

A Reading (Lesson) from the Book of Exodus [3:11-15]

Moses said to God, "Who am I that I should go to Pharaoh, and bring the sons of Israel out of Egypt?" He said, "But I will be with you; and this shall be the sign for you, that I have sent you: when you have brought forth the people out of Egypt, you shall serve God upon this mountain." Then Moses said to God, "If I come to the people of Israel and say to them, 'The God of your fathers has sent me to you,' and they ask me, 'What is his name?' what shall I say to them?" God said to Moses, "I am who I am." And he said, "Say this to the people of Israel, 'I am has sent me to you.' " God also said to Moses, "Say this to the people of Israel, 'The Lord, the God of your fathers, the God of Abraham, the God of Isaac, and the God of Jacob, has sent me to you': this is my name for ever, and thus I am to be remembered throughout all generations."

Psalm 29 [page 620]

*A Reading (Lesson) from the Letter of Paul
to the Romans* [11:33-36]

O the depth of the riches and wisdom and knowledge of
God! How unsearchable are his judgments and how
inscrutable his ways! "For who has known the mind of the
Lord, or who has been his counselor?" "Or who has given
a gift to him that he might be repaid?" For from him and
through him and to him are all things. To him be glory for
ever. Amen.

✝ *The Holy Gospel of Our Lord Jesus Christ
According to Matthew* [28:18-20]

Jesus came and said to the eleven disciples, "All authority
in heaven and on earth has been given to me. Go therefore
and make disciples of all nations, baptizing them in the
name of the Father and of the Son and of the Holy Spirit,
teaching them to observe all that I have commanded you;
and lo, I am with you always, to the close of the age."

2. Of the Holy Spirit

A Reading (Lesson) from the Book of Isaiah [61:1-3]

The Spirit of the Lord God is upon me, because the Lord
has annointed me to bring good tidings to the afflicted; he
has sent me to bind up the brokenhearted, to proclaim
liberty to the captives, and the opening of the prison to
those who are bound; to proclaim the year of the Lord's
favor, and the day of vengeance of our God; to comfort all
who mourn; to grant to those who mourn in Zion — to
give them a garland instead of ashes, the oil of gladness

instead of mourning, the mantle of praise instead of a faint spirit; that they may be called oaks of righteousness, the planting of the Lord, that he may be glorified.

Psalm 139:1-9(10-17) [page 794]

A Reading (Lesson) from the First Letter of Paul to the Corinthians [12:4-14]

There are varieties of gifts, but the same Spirit; and there are varieties of service, but the same Lord; and there are varieties of working, but it is the same God who inspires them all in every one. To each is given the manifestation of the Spirit for the common good. To one is given through the Spirit the utterance of wisdom, and to another the utterance of knowledge according to the same Spirit, to another faith by the same Spirit, to another gifts of healing by the one Spirit, to another the working of miracles, to another prophecy, to another the ability to distinguish between spirits, to another various kinds of tongues, to another the interpretation of tongues. All these are inspired by one and the same Spirit, who apportions to each one individually as he wills. For just as the body is one and has many members, and all the members of the body, though many, are one body, so it is with Christ. For by one Spirit we are all baptized into one body — Jews or Greeks, slaves or free — and all were made to drink of one Spirit. For the body does not consist of one member but of many.

✝ *The Holy Gospel of Our Lord Jesus Christ According to Luke* [11:9-13]

Jesus said to his disciples, "I tell you, Ask, and it will be given you; seek, and you will find; knock, and it will be opened to you. For every one who asks receives, and he who seeks finds, and to him who knocks it will be opened.

What father among you, if his son asks for a fish, will instead of a fish give him a serpent; or if he asks for an egg, will give him a scorpion? If you then, who are evil, know how to give good gifts to your children, how much more will the heavenly Father give the Holy Spirit to those who ask him!"

3. Of the Holy Angels

A Reading (Lesson) from the Book of Daniel [7:9-10a]

As I looked, thrones were placed and one that was ancient of days took his seat; his raiment was white as snow, and the hair of his head like pure wool; his throne was fiery flames, its wheels were burning fire. A stream of fire issued and came forth from before him; a thousand thousands served him, and ten thousand times ten thousand stood before him.

or this

A Reading (Lesson) from the Second Book of the Kings [6:8-17]

Once when the king of Syria was warring against Israel, he took counsel with his servants, saying, "At such and such a place shall be my camp." But the man of God sent word to the king of Israel, "Beware that you do not pass this place, for the Syrians are going down there." And the king of Israel sent to the place of which the man of God told him. Thus he used to warn him, so that he saved himself there more than once or twice. And the mind of the king of Syria was greatly troubled because of this thing; and he called his servants and said to them, "Will you not show me who of us is for the king of Israel?" And one of his servants said, "None, my lord, O king; but Eli'sha, the prophet who is in Israel, tells the king of Israel the words that you speak in your bedchamber." And he said, "Go and see where he is, that I may send and seize him." It was told him, "Behold, he is in Dothan." So he sent there horses and chariots and a great army; and they came by night, and surrounded the city. When the servant of the man of God rose early in the morning and went out, behold, an army with horses and chariots was round about the city. And the servant said, "Alas, my master! What shall we do?" He said, "Fear not, for those who are with us are more than those who are with them." Then Eli'sha prayed, and said, "Lord, I pray thee, open his eyes that he may see." So the Lord opened the eyes of the young man, and he saw; and behold, the mountain was full of horses and chariots of fire around Eli'sha.

Psalm 148 [page 805]   or   *Psalm 103:19-22* [page 734]

A Reading (Lesson) from the Revelation to John
[5:11-14]

I looked, and I heard around the throne and the living creatures and the elders the voice of many angels, numbering myriads of myriads and thousands of thousands, saying with a loud voice, "Worthy is the Lamb who was slain, to receive power and wealth and wisdom and might and honor and glory and blessing!" And I heard every creature in heaven and on earth and under the earth and in the sea, and all therein, saying, "To him who sits upon the throne and to the Lamb be blessing and honor and glory and might for ever and ever!" And the four living creatures said, "Amen!" and the elders fell down and worshiped.

✝ *The Holy Gospel of Our Lord Jesus Christ According to John* [1:47-51]

Jesus saw Nathan′a-el coming to him, and said of him, "Behold, an Israelite indeed, in whom is no guile!" Nathan′a-el said to him, "How do you know me?" Jesus answered him, "Before Philip called you, when you were under the fig tree, I saw you." Nathan′a-el answered him, "Rabbi, you are the Son of God! You are the King of Israel!" Jesus answered him, "Because I said to you I saw you under the fig tree, do you believe? You shall see greater things than these." And he said to him, "Truly, truly, I say to you, you will see heaven opened, and the angels of God ascending and descending upon the Son of man."

4. Of the Incarnation

A Reading (Lesson) from the Book of Isaiah [11:1-10]

There shall come forth a shoot from the stump of Jesse, and a branch shall grow out of his roots. And the Spirit of the Lord shall rest upon him, the spirit of wisdom and understanding, the spirit of counsel and might, the spirit of knowledge and the fear of the Lord. And his delight shall be in the fear of the Lord. He shall not judge by what his eyes see, or decide by what his ears hear; but with righteousness he shall judge the poor, and decide with equity for the meek of the earth; and he shall smite the earth with the rod of his mouth, and with the breath of his lips he shall slay the wicked. Righteousness shall be the girdle of his waist, and faithfulness the girdle of his loins.

The wolf shall dwell with the lamb, and the leopard shall lie down with the kid, and the calf and the lion and the fatling together, and a little child shall lead them. The cow and the bear shall feed; their young shall lie down together; and the lion shall eat straw like the ox. The sucking child shall play over the hole of the asp, and the weaned child shall put his hand on the adder's den. They shall not hurt or destroy in all my holy mountain; for the earth shall be full of the knowledge of the Lord as the waters cover the sea. In that day the root of Jesse shall stand as an ensign to the peoples; him shall the nations seek, and his dwellings shall be glorious.

or this

A Reading (Lesson) from the Book of Genesis [17:1-8]

When Abram was ninety-nine years old the Lord appeared to Abram, and said to him, "I am God Almighty; walk before me, and be blameless. And I will make my covenant between me and you, and will multiply you exceedingly." Then Abram fell on his face; and God said to him, "Behold, my covenant is with you, and you shall be the father of a multitude of nations. No longer shall your name be Abram, but your name shall be Abraham; for I have made you the father of a multitude of nations. I will make you exceedingly fruitful; and I will make nations of you, and kings shall come forth from you. And I will establish my covenant between me and you and your descendants after you throughout their generations for an everlasting covenant, to be God to you and to your descendants after you. And I will give to you, and to your descendants after you, the land of your sojournings, all the land of Canaan, for an everlasting possession; and I will be their God."

Psalm 111 [page 754]   or   *Psalm 132:11-19* [page 786]

A Reading (Lesson) from the First Letter of John [4:1-11]

Beloved, do not believe every spirit, but test the spirits to see whether they are of God; for many false prophets have gone out into the world. By this you know the Spirit of God: every spirit which confesses that Jesus Christ has come in the flesh is of God, and every spirit which does not confess Jesus is not of God. This is the spirit of antichrist, of which you heard that it was coming, and now it is in the world already. Little children, you are of God, and have overcome them; for he who is in you is greater than he who is in the world. They are of the world, therefore what they say is of the world, and the world listens to them. We are of God. Whoever knows God listens to us, and he who is not of God does not listen to us. By this we know the spirit of truth and the spirit of error. Beloved, let us love one another; for love is of God, and he who loves is born of God and knows God. He who does not love does not know God; for God is love. In this the love of God was made manifest among us, that God sent his only Son into the world, so that we might live through him. In this is love, not that we loved God but that he loved us and sent his Son to be the expiation for our sins. Beloved, if God so loved us, we also ought to love one another.

or this

A Reading (Lesson) from the First Letter of Paul to Timothy [3:14-16]

I hope to come to you soon, but I am writing these instructions to you so that, if I am delayed, you may know how one ought to behave in the household of God, which is the church of the living God, the pillar and bulwark of the truth. Great indeed, we confess, is the mystery of our religion: He was manifested in the flesh, vindicated in the Spirit, seen by angels, preached among the nations, believed on in the world, taken up in glory.

✝ *The Holy Gospel of Our Lord Jesus Christ According to Luke* [1:26-33(34-38)]

In the sixth month the angel Gabriel was sent from God to a city of Galilee named Nazareth, to a virgin betrothed to a man whose name was Joseph, of the house of David; and the virgin's name was Mary. And he came to her and said, "Hail, O favored one, the Lord is with you!" But she was greatly troubled at the saying, and considered in her mind what sort of greeting this might be. And the angel said to her, "Do not be afraid, Mary, for you have found favor with God. And behold, you will conceive in your womb and bear a son, and you shall call his name Jesus. He will be great, and will be called the Son of the Most High; and the Lord God will give to him the throne of his father David, and he will reign over the house of Jacob for ever; and of his kingdom there will be no end."

And Mary said to the angel, "How shall this be, since I have no husband?" And the angel said to her, "The Holy Spirit will come upon you, and the power of the Most High will overshadow you; therefore the child to be born will be called holy, the Son of God. And behold, your kinswoman Elizabeth in her old age has also conceived a son; and this is the sixth month with her who was called barren. For with God nothing will be impossible." And Mary said, "Behold, I am the handmaid of the Lord; let it be to me according to your word." And the angel departed from her.

or the following

✝ *The Holy Gospel of Our Lord Jesus Christ*
According to Luke [11:27-28]

As Jesus spoke, a woman in the crowd raised her voice and said to him, "Blessed is the womb that bore you, and the breasts that you sucked!" But he said, "Blessed rather are those who hear the word of God and keep it!"

5. Of the Holy Eucharist

A Reading (Lesson) from the Book of Deuteronomy
[8:2-3]

Moses said to the people, "You shall remember all the ways which the Lord your God has led you these forty years in the wilderness, that he might humble you, testing you to know what was in your heart, whether you would keep his commandments, or not. And he humbled you and let you hunger and fed you with manna, which you did not know, nor did your fathers know; that he might make you know that man does not live by bread alone, but that man lives by everything that proceeds out of the mouth of the Lord."

Psalm 34 [page 627]   or   *Psalm 116:10-17* [page 759]

A Reading (Lesson) from the Revelation to John
[19:1-2a,4-9]

I heard what seemed to be the loud voice of a great multitude in heaven, crying, "Hallelujah! Salvation and glory and power belong to our God, for his judgments are true and just. And the twenty-four elders and the four living creatures fell down and worshiped God who is

seated on the throne, saying "Amen. Hallelujah!" And
from the throne came a voice crying, "Praise our God, all
you his servants, you who fear him, small and great."
Then I heard what seemed to be the voice of a great
multitude, like the sound of many waters and like the
sound of mighty thunderpeals, crying, "Hallelujah! For
the Lord our God the Almighty reigns. Let us rejoice and
exult and give him the glory, for the marriage of the Lamb
has come, and his Bride has made herself ready; it was
granted her to be clothed with fine linen, bright and pure"
— for the fine linen is the righteous deeds of the saints.
And the angel said to me, "Write this: Blessed are those
who are invited to the marriage supper of the Lamb." And
he said to me, "These are true words of God."

or this

A Reading (Lesson) from the First Letter of Paul to the Corinthians [10:1-4,16-17]

I want you to know, brethren, that our fathers were all
under the cloud, and all passed through the sea, and all
were baptized into Moses in the cloud and in the sea, and
all ate the same supernatural food and all drank the same
supernatural drink. For they drank from the Rock which
followed them, and the Rock was Christ. The cup of
blessing which we bless, is it not a participation in the
blood of Christ? The bread which we break, is it not a
participation in the body of Christ? Because there is one
bread, we who are many are one body, for we all partake
of the one bread.

or the following

*A Reading (Lesson) from the First Letter of Paul
to the Corinthians* [11:23-29]

I received from the Lord what I also delivered to you, that
the Lord Jesus on the night when he was betrayed took
bread, and when he had given thanks, he broke it, and
said, "This is my body which is for you. Do this in
remembrance of me." In the same way also the cup, after
supper, saying, "This cup is the new covenant in my
blood. Do this, as often as you drink it, in remembrance of
me." For as often as you eat this bread and drink the cup,
you proclaim the Lord's death until he comes. Whoever,
therefore, eats the bread or drinks the cup of the Lord in
an unworthy manner will be guilty of profaning the body
and blood of the Lord. Let a man examine himself, and so
eat of the bread and drink of the cup. For any one who
eats and drinks without discerning the body eats and
drinks judgment upon himself.

✝ *The Holy Gospel of Our Lord Jesus Christ
According to John* [6:47-58]

Jesus said to the people, "Truly, truly, I say to you, he
who believes has eternal life. I am the bread of life. Your
fathers ate the manna in the wilderness, and they died.
This is the bread which comes down from heaven, that a
man may eat of it and not die. I am the living bread which
came down from heaven; if any one eats of this bread, he
will live for ever; and the bread which I shall give for the
life of the world is my flesh." The Jews then disputed
among themselves, saying, "How can this man give us his
flesh to eat?" So Jesus said to them, "Truly, truly, I say to
you, unless you eat the flesh of the Son of man and drink
his blood, you have no life in you; he who eats my flesh
and drinks my blood has eternal life, and I will raise him
up at the last day. For my flesh is food indeed, and my

blood is drink indeed. He who eats my flesh and drinks my blood abides in me, and I in him. As the living Father sent me, and I live because of the Father, so he who eats me will live because of me. This is the bread which came down from heaven, not such as the fathers ate and died; he who eats this bread will live for ever."

6. Of the Holy Cross

A Reading (Lesson) from the Book of Isaiah
[52:13-15;53:10-12]

Behold, my servant shall prosper, he shall be exalted and lifted up, and shall be very high. As many were astonished at him — his appearance was so marred, beyond human semblance, and his form beyond that of the sons of men — so shall he startle many nations; kings shall shut their mouths because of him; for that which has not been told them they shall see, and that which they have not heard they shall understand. Yet it was the will of the Lord to bruise him; he has put him to grief; when he makes himself an offering for sin, he shall see his offspring, he shall prolong his days; the will of the Lord shall prosper in his hand; he shall see the fruit of the travail of his soul and be satisfied; by his knowledge shall the righteous one, my servant, make many to be accounted righteous; and he shall bear their iniquities. Therefore I will divide him a portion with the great, and he shall divide the spoil with the strong; because he poured out his soul to death, and was numbered with the transgressors; yet he bore the sin of many, and made intercession for the transgressors.

Psalm 40:(1-4)5-11 [page 640]

*A Reading (Lesson) from the First Letter of Paul
to the Corinthians* [1:18-24]

The word of the cross is folly to those who are perishing,
but to us who are being saved it is the power of God. For it
is written, "I will destroy the wisdom of the wise, and the
cleverness of the clever I will thwart." Where is your wise
man? Where is the scribe? Where is the debater of this age?
Has not God made foolish the wisdom of the world? For
since, in the wisdom of God, the world did not know God
through wisdom, it pleased God through the folly of what
we preach to save those who believe. For Jews demand
signs and Greeks seek wisdom, but we preach Christ
crucified, a stumbling block to Jews and folly to Gentiles,
but to those who are called, both Jews and Greeks, Christ
the power of God and the wisdom of God.

✝ *The Holy Gospel of Our Lord Jesus Christ
According to John* [12:23-33]

Jesus said to Andrew and Philip, "The hour has come for
the Son of man to be glorified. Truly, truly, I say to you,
unless a grain of wheat falls into the earth and dies, it
remains alone, but if it dies, it bears much fruit. He who
loves his life loses it, and he who hates his life in this world
will keep it for eternal life. If any one serves me, he must
follow me; and where I am, there shall my servant be also;
if any one serves me, the Father will honor him. Now is my
soul troubled. And what shall I say? 'Father, save me from
this hour'? No, for this purpose I have come to this hour.
Father, glorify thy name." Then a voice came from heaven,
"I have glorified it, and I will glorify it again." The crowd
standing by heard it and said that it had thundered. Others
said, "An angel has spoken to him." Jesus answered, "This
voice has come for your sake, not for mine. Now is the
judgment of this world, now shall the ruler of this world be

cast out; and I, when I am lifted up from the earth, will draw all men to myself." He said this to show by what death he was to die.

7. For All Baptized Christians

A Reading (Lesson) from the Book of Jeremiah [17:7-8]

Thus says the Lord: "Blessed is the man who trusts in the Lord, whose trust is the Lord. He is like a tree planted by water, that sends out its roots by the stream, and does not fear when heat comes, for its leaves remain green, and is not anxious in the year of drought, for it does not cease to bear fruit."

or this

A Reading (Lesson) from the Book of Ezekiel [36:24-28]

Thus says the Lord God: "I will take you from the nations, and gather you from all the countries, and bring you into your own land. I will sprinkle clean water upon you, and you shall be clean from all your uncleannesses, and from all your idols I will cleanse you. A new heart I will give you, and a new spirit I will put within you; and I will take out of your flesh the heart of stone and give you a heart of flesh. And I will put my spirit within you, and cause you to walk in my statutes and be careful to observe my ordinances. You shall dwell in the land which I gave to your fathers; and you shall be my people, and I will be your God."

Psalm 16:5-11 [page 600]

*A Reading (Lesson) from the Letter of Paul
to the Romans* [6:3-11]

Do you not know that all of us who have been baptized
into Christ Jesus were baptized into his death? We were
buried therefore with him by baptism into death, so that as
Christ was raised from the dead by the glory of the Father,
we too might walk in newness of life. For if we have been
united with him in a death like his, we shall certainly be
united with him in a resurrection like his. We know that
our old self was crucified with him so that the sinful body
might be destroyed, and we might no longer be enslaved to
sin. For he who has died is freed from sin. But if we have
died with Christ, we believe that we shall also live with
him. For we know that Christ being raised from the dead
will never die again; death no longer has dominion over
him. The death he died he died to sin, once for all, but the
life he lives he lives to God. So you also must consider
yourselves dead to sin and alive to God in Christ Jesus.

✝ *The Holy Gospel of Our Lord Jesus Christ
According to Mark* [10:35-45]

James and John, the sons of Zeb'edee, came forward to
Jesus, and said to him, "Teacher, we want you to do for us
whatever we ask of you." And he said to them, "What do
you want me to do for you?" And they said to him, "Grant
us to sit, one at your right hand and one at your left, in
your glory." But Jesus said to them, "You do not know
what you are asking. Are you able to drink the cup that I
drink, or to be baptized with the baptism with which I am
baptized?" And they said to him, "We are able." And Jesus
said to them, "The cup that I drink you will drink; and
with the baptism with which I am baptized, you will be
baptized; but to sit at my right hand or at my left is not
mine to grant, but it is for those for whom it has been

prepared." And when the ten heard it, they began to be indignant at James and John. And Jesus called them to him and said to them, "You know that those who are supposed to rule over the Gentiles lord it over them, and their great men exercise authority over them. But it shall not be so among you; but whoever would be great among you must be your servant, and whoever would be first among you must be slave of all. For the Son of man also came not to be served but to serve, and to give his life as a ransom for many."

8. For the Departed
[pages 76-77 above]

9. Of the Reign of Christ

A Reading (Lesson) from the Book of Daniel [7:9-14]

As I looked, thrones were placed and one that was ancient of days took his seat; his raiment was white as snow, and the hair of his head like pure wool; his throne was fiery flames, its wheels were burning fire. A stream of fire issued and came forth from before him, a thousand thousands served him, and ten thousand times ten thousand stood before him; the court sat in judgment, and the books were opened. I looked then because of the sound of the great words which the horn was speaking. And as I looked, the beast was slain, and its body destroyed and given over to be burned with fire. As for the rest of the beasts, their dominion was taken away, but their lives were prolonged for a season and a time. I saw in the night visions, and behold, with the clouds of heaven there came one like a son of man, and he came to the Ancient of Days and was presented before him. And to him was given dominion and glory and kingdom, that all peoples, nations, and languages should serve him; his dominion is an everlasting dominion, which shall not pass away, and his kingdom one that shall not be destroyed.

Psalm 93 [page 722]   or   *Canticle 18* [page 93]

A Reading (Lesson) from the Letter of Paul to the Colossians [1:11-20]

May you be strengthened with all power, according to his glorious might, for all endurance and patience with joy, giving thanks to the Father, who has qualified us to share in the inheritance of the saints in light. He has delivered us from the dominion of darkness and transferred us to the kingdom of his beloved Son, in whom we have redemption, the forgiveness of sins. He is the image of the invisible God, the first-born of all creation; for in him all things were created, in heaven and on earth, visible and invisible, whether thrones or dominions or principalities or authorities — all things were created through him and for him. He is before all things, and in him all things hold together. He is the head of the body, the church; he is the beginning, the first-born from the dead, that in everything he might be pre-eminent. For in him all the fulness of God was pleased to dwell, and through him to reconcile to himself all things, whether on earth or in heaven, making peace by the blood of his cross.

✝ *The Holy Gospel of Our Lord Jesus Christ*
According to John [18:33-37]

Pilate entered the praetorium again and called Jesus, and said to him, "Are you the King of the Jews?" Jesus answered, "Do you say this of your own accord, or did others say it to you about me?" Pilate answered, "Am I a Jew? Your own nation and the chief priests have handed you over to me; what have you done?" Jesus answered, "My kingdom is not of this world; if my kingship were of this world, my servants would fight, that I might not be handed over to the Jews; but my kingship is not from the world." Pilate said to him, "So you are a king?" Jesus answered, "You say that I am a king. For this I was born, and for this I have come into the world, to bear witness to the truth. Every one who is of the truth hears my voice."

Any of the Psalms and Lessons appointed in Proper 29 may be used instead.

10. At Baptism
[pages 20-21 above]

11. At Confirmation
[pages 25-32 above]

12. Anniversary of the Dedication of a Church

A Reading (Lesson) from the First Book of the Kings
[8:22-30]

Solomon stood before the altar of the Lord in the presence of all the assembly of Israel, and spread forth his hands toward heaven; and said, "O Lord, God of Israel, there is no God like thee, in heaven above or on earth beneath, keeping covenant and showing steadfast love to thy servants who walk before thee with all their heart; who hast kept with thy servant David my father what thou didst declare to him; yea, thou didst speak with thy mouth, and with thy hand hast fulfilled it this day. Now therefore, O Lord, God of Israel, keep with thy servant David my father what thou hast promised him, saying, 'There shall never fail you a man before me to sit upon the throne of Israel, if only your sons take heed to their way, to walk before me as you have walked before me,' Now therefore, O God of Israel, let thy word be confirmed, which thou hast spoken to thy servant David my father. But will God indeed dwell on the earth? Behold, heaven and the highest heaven cannot contain thee; how much less this house which I have built! Yet have regard to the prayer of thy servant and to his supplication, O Lord my God, hearkening to the cry and to the prayer which thy servant prays before thee this day; that thy eyes may be open night and day toward this house, the place of which thou hast said, 'My name shall be there,' that thou mayest hearken to the prayer which thy servant offers toward this place. And hearken thou to the supplication of thy servant and of thy people Israel, when they pray toward this place; yea, hear thou in heaven thy dwelling place; and when thou hearest, forgive."

or this

A Reading (Lesson) from the Book of Genesis [28:10-17]

Jacob left Beer-sheba, and went toward Haran. And he came to a certain place, and stayed there that night, because the sun had set. Taking one of the stones of the place, he put it under his head and lay down in that place to sleep. And he dreamed that there was a ladder set up on the earth, and the top of it reached to heaven; and behold, the angels of God were ascending and descending on it! And behold, the Lord stood above it and said, "I am the Lord, the God of Abraham your father and the God of Isaac; the land on which you lie I will give to you and to your descendants; and your descendants shall be like the dust of the earth, and you shall spread abroad to the west and to the east and to the north and to the south; and by you and your descendants shall all the families of the earth bless themselves. Behold, I am with you and will keep you wherever you go, and will bring you back to this land; for I will not leave you until I have done that of which I have spoken to you." Then Jacob awoke from his sleep and said, "Surely the Lord is in this place; and I did not know it." And he was afraid, and said, "How awesome is this place! This is none other than the house of God, and this is the gate of heaven."

Psalm 84:1-6(7-12) [page 707]

A Reading (Lesson) from the First Letter of Peter
[2:1-5,9-10]

Put away all malice and all guile and insincerity and envy and all slander. Like newborn babes, long for the pure spiritual milk, that by it you may grow up into salvation; for you have tasted the kindness of the Lord. Come to him, to that living stone, rejected by men but in God's sight chosen and precious; and like living stones be yourselves built into a spiritual house, to be a holy priesthood, to offer spiritual sacrifices acceptable to God through Jesus Christ. But you are a chosen race, a royal priesthood, a holy nation, God's own people, that you may declare the wonderful deeds of him who called you out of darkness into his marvelous light.

✠ *The Holy Gospel of Our Lord Jesus Christ According to Matthew* [21:12-16]

Jesus entered the temple of God and drove out all who sold and bought in the temple, and he overturned the tables of the moneychangers and the seats of those who sold pigeons. He said to them, "It is written, 'My house shall be called a house of prayer'; but you make it a den of robbers." And the blind and the lame came to him in the temple, and he healed them. But when the chief priests and the scribes saw the wonderful things he did, and the children crying out in the temple, "Hosanna to the Son of David!" they were indignant; and they said to him, "Do you hear what these are saying?" And Jesus said to them, "Yes; have you never read, 'Out of the mouth of babes and sucklings thou hast brought perfect praise'?"

13. For a Church Convention

A Reading (Lesson) from the Book of Isaiah [55:1-13]

Thus says the Lord: "Ho, every one who thirsts, come to the waters; and he who has no money, come, buy and eat! Come, buy wine and milk without money and without price. Why do you spend your money for that which is not bread, and your labor for that which does not satisfy? Hearken diligently to me, and eat what is good, and delight yourselves in fatness. Incline your ear, and come to me; hear, that your soul may live; and I will make with you an everlasting covenant, my steadfast, sure love for David. Behold, I made him a witness to the peoples, a leader and commander for the peoples. Behold, you shall call nations that you know not, and nations that knew you not shall run to you, because of the Lord your God, and of the Holy One of Israel, for he has glorified you. Seek the Lord while he may be found, call upon him while he is near; let the wicked forsake his way, and the unrighteous man his thoughts; let him return to the Lord, that he may have mercy on him, and to our God, for he will abundantly pardon. For my thoughts are not your thoughts, neither are your ways my ways, says the Lord. For as the heavens are higher than the earth, so are my ways higher than your ways and my thoughts than your thoughts. For as the rain and the snow come down from heaven, and return not thither but water the earth, making it bring forth and sprout, giving seed to the sower and bread to the eater, so shall my word be that goes forth from my mouth; it shall not return to me empty, but it shall accomplish that which I purpose, and prosper in the thing for which I sent it. For you shall go out in joy, and be led forth in peace; the mountains and the hills before you shall break forth into singing, and all the trees of the field shall clap their hands. Instead of the thorn shall come up the cypress; instead of the brier shall come up the myrtle; and it shall be to the Lord for a memorial, for an everlasting sign which shall not be cut off."

Psalm 19:7-14 [page 607]

A Reading (Lesson) from the Second Letter of Paul to the Corinthians [4:1-10]

Having this ministry by the mercy of God, we do not lose heart. We have renounced disgraceful, underhanded ways; we refuse to practice cunning or to tamper with God's word, but by the open statement of the truth we would commend ourselves to every man's conscience in the sight of God. And even if our gospel is veiled, it is veiled only to those who are perishing. In their case the god of this world has blinded the minds of the unbelievers, to keep them from seeing the light of the gospel of the glory of Christ, who is the likeness of God. For what we preach is not ourselves, but Jesus Christ as Lord, with ourselves as your servants for Jesus' sake. For it is the God who said, "Let light shine out of darkness," who has shone in our hearts to give the light of the knowledge of the glory of God in the face of Christ. But we have this treasure in earthen vessels, to show that the transcendent power belongs to God and not to us. We are afflicted in every way, but not crushed; perplexed, but not driven to despair; persecuted, but not forsaken; struck down, but not destroyed; always carrying in the body the death of Jesus, so that the life of Jesus may also be manifested in our bodies.

✝ *The Holy Gospel of Our Lord Jesus Christ According to John* [15:1-11]

Jesus said, "I am the true vine, and my father is the vinedresser. Every branch of mine that bears no fruit, he takes away, and every branch that does bear fruit he prunes, that it may bear more fruit. You are already made clean by the word which I have spoken to you. Abide in me, and I in you. As the branch cannot bear fruit by itself, unless it abides in the vine, neither can you, unless you abide in me. I am the vine, you are the branches. He who abides in me, and I in him, he it is that bears much fruit, for apart from me you can do nothing. If a man does not abide in me, he is cast forth as a branch and withers; and the branches are gathered, thrown into the fire and burned. If you abide in me, and my words abide in you, ask whatever you will, and it shall be done for you. By this my Father is glorified, that you bear much fruit, and so prove to be my disciples. As the Father has loved me, so have I loved you; abide in my love. If you keep my commandments, you will abide in my love, just as I have kept my Father's commandments and abide in his love. These things I have spoken to you, that my joy may be in you, and that your joy may be full."

14. For the Unity of the Church

A Reading (Lesson) from the Book of Isaiah [35:1-10]

The wilderness and the dry land shall be glad, the desert shall rejoice and blossom; like the crocus it shall blossom abundantly, and rejoice with joy and singing. The glory of Lebanon shall be given to it, the majesty of Carmel and

Sharon. They shall see the glory of the Lord, the majesty of our God. Strengthen the weak hands, and make firm the feeble knees. Say to those who are of a fearful heart, "Be strong, fear not! Behold, your God will come with vengeance, with the recompense of God. He will come and save you." Then the eyes of the blind shall be opened, and the ears of the deaf unstopped; then shall the lame man leap like a hart, and the tongue of the dumb sing for joy. For waters shall break forth in the wilderness, and streams in the desert; the burning sand shall become a pool, and the thirsty ground springs of water; the haunt of jackals shall become a swamp, the grass shall become reeds and rushes. And a highway shall be there, and it shall be called the Holy Way; the unclean shall not pass over it, and fools shall not err therein. No lion shall be there, nor shall any ravenous beast come upon it; they shall not be found there, but the redeemed shall walk there. And the ransomed of the Lord shall return, and come to Zion with singing; everlasting joy shall be upon their heads; they shall obtain joy and gladness, and sorrow and sighing shall flee away.

Psalm 122 [page 779]

A Reading (Lesson) from the Letter of Paul to the Ephesians [4:1-6]

I therefore, a prisoner for the Lord, beg you to lead a life worthy of the calling to which you have been called, with all lowliness and meekness, with patience, forbearing one another in love, eager to maintain the unity of the Spirit in the bond of peace. There is one body and one Spirit, just as you were called to the one hope that belongs to your call, one Lord, one faith, one baptism, one God and Father of us all, who is above all and through all and in all.

✝ *The Holy Gospel of Our Lord Jesus Christ*
According to John [17:6a,15-23]

Jesus said, "I have manifested thy name to the men whom thou gavest me out of the world. I do not pray that thou shouldst take them out of the world, but that thou shouldst keep them from the evil one. They are not of the world, even as I am not of the world. Sanctify them in the truth; thy word is truth. As thou didst send me into the world, so I have sent them into the world. And for their sake I consecrate myself, that they also may be consecrated in truth. I do not pray for these only, but also for those who believe in me through their word, that they may all be one; even as thou, Father, art in me, and I in thee, that they also may be in us, so that the world may believe that thou hast sent me. The glory which thou hast given me I have given to them, that they may be one even as we are one, I in them and thou in me, that they may become perfectly one, so that the world may know that thou hast sent me and hast loved them even as thou hast loved me."

15. For the Ministry I

A Reading (Lesson) from the Book of Numbers
[11:16-17,24-29]

The Lord said to Moses, "Gather for me seventy men of the elders of Israel, whom you know to be the elders of the people and officers over them; and bring them to the tent of meeting, and let them take their stand there with you. And I will come down and talk with you there; and I will take some of the spirit which is upon you and put it upon them; and they shall bear the burden of the people with you, that you may not bear it yourself alone." So Moses went out and told the people the words of the Lord; and he gathered seventy men of the elders of the people, and placed them round about the tent. Then the Lord came down in the cloud and spoke to him, and took some of the spirit that was upon him and put it upon the seventy elders; and when the spirit rested upon them, they prophesied. But they did so no more. Now two men remained in the camp, one named Eldad, and the other named Medad, and the spirit rested upon them; they were among those registered, but they had not gone out to the tent, and so they prophesied in the camp. And a young man ran and told Moses, "Eldad and Medad are prophesying in the camp." And Joshua the son of Nun, the minister of Moses, one of his chosen men, said, "My lord Moses, forbid them." But Moses said to him, "Are you jealous for my sake? Would that all the Lord's people were prophets, that the Lord would put his spirit upon them!"

Psalm 99 [page 728] or *Psalm 27:1-9* [page 617]

A Reading (Lesson) from the First Letter of Paul to the Corinthians [3:5-11]

What then is Apol'los? What is Paul? Servants through whom you believed, as the Lord assigned to each. I planted, Apol'los watered, but God gave the growth. So neither he who plants nor he who waters is anything, but only God who gives the growth. He who plants and he who waters are equal, and each shall receive his wages according to his labor. For we are God's fellow workers; you are God's field, God's building. According to the grace of God given to me, like a skilled master builder I laid a foundation, and another man is building upon it.

Let each man take care how he builds upon it. For no other foundation can any one lay than that which is laid, which is Christ Jesus.

✝ *The Holy Gospel of Our Lord Jesus Christ According to John* [4:31-38]

The disciples besought Jesus, saying, "Rabbi, eat." But he said to them , "I have food to eat of which you do not know." So the disciples said to one another, "Has any one brought him food?" Jesus said to them, "My food is to do the will of him who sent me, and to accomplish his work. Do you not say, 'There are yet four months, then comes the harvest'? I tell you, lift up your eyes, and see how the fields are already white for harvest. He who reaps receives wages, and gathers fruit for eternal life, so that sower and reaper may rejoice together. For here the saying holds true, 'One sows and another reaps.' I sent you to reap that for which you did not labor; others have labored, and you have entered into their labor."

15. For the Ministry II

A Reading (Lesson) from the First Book of Samuel [3:1-10]

The boy Samuel was ministering to the Lord under Eli. And the word of the Lord was rare in those days; there was no frequent vision. At that time Eli, whose eyesight had begun to grow dim, so that he could not see, was lying down in his own place; the lamp of God had not yet gone out, and Samuel was lying down within the temple of the Lord, where the ark of God was. Then the Lord called,

"Samuel! Samuel!" and he said, "Here I am!" and ran to
Eli, and said, "Here I am, for you called me." But he said,
"I did not call; lie down again." So he went and lay down.
And the Lord called again, "Samuel!" And Samuel arose
and went to Eli, and said, "Here I am, for you called me."
But he said, "I did not call, my son; lie down again." Now
Samuel did not yet know the Lord, and the word of the
Lord had not yet been revealed to him. And the Lord
called Samuel again the third time. And he arose and went
to Eli, and said, "Here I am, for you called me." Then Eli
perceived that the Lord was calling the boy. Therefore Eli
said to Samuel, "Go, lie down, and if he calls you, you
shall say, 'Speak, Lord, for thy servant hears.' " So Samuel
went and lay down in his place. And the Lord came and
stood forth, calling as at other times, "Samuel! Samuel!"
And Samuel said, "Speak, for thy servant hears."

Psalm 63:1-8 [page 670]

*A Reading (Lesson) from the Letter of Paul
to the Ephesians* [4:11-16]

The Spirit's gifts were that some should be apostles, some
prophets, some evangelists, some pastors and teachers, to
equip the saints for the work of ministry, for building up
the body of Christ, until we all attain to the unity of the
faith and of the knowledge of the Son of God, to mature
manhood, to the measure of the stature of the fulness of
Christ; so that we may no longer be children, tossed to
and fro and carried about with every kind of doctrine, by
the cunning of men, by their craftiness in deceitful wiles.
Rather, speaking the truth in love, we are to grow up in
every way into him who is the head, into Christ, from
whom the whole body, joined and knit together by every
joint with which it is supplied, when each part is working
properly, makes bodily growth and upbuilds itself in love.

✝ *The Holy Gospel of Our Lord Jesus Christ*
According to Matthew [9:35-38]

Jesus went about all the cities and villages, teaching in the synagogues and preaching the gospel of the kingdom, and healing every disease and every infirmity. When he saw the crowds, he had compassion for them, because they were harassed and helpless, like sheep without a shepherd. Then he said to his disciples, "The harvest is plentiful, but the laborers are few; pray therefore the Lord of the harvest to send out laborers into his harvest."

15. For the Ministry III

A Reading (Lesson) from the Book of Exodus [19:3-8]

Moses went up to God, and the Lord called to him out of the mountain, saying, "Thus you shall say to the house of Jacob, and tell the people of Israel: You have seen what I did to the Egyptians, and how I bore you on eagles' wings and brought you to myself. Now therefore, if you will obey my voice and keep my covenant, you shall be my own possession among all peoples; for all the earth is mine, and you shall be to me a kingdom of priests and a holy nation. These are the words which you shall speak to the children of Israel." So Moses came and called the elders of the people, and set before them all these words which the Lord had commanded him. And all the people answered together and said, "All that the Lord has spoken we will do." And Moses reported the words of the people to the Lord.

Psalm 15 [page 599]

A Reading (Lesson) from the First Letter of Peter [4:7-11]

The end of all things is at hand; therefore keep sane and sober for your prayers. Above all hold unfailing your love for one another since love covers a multitude of sins. Practice hospitality ungrudgingly to one another. As each has received a gift, employ it for one another, as good stewards of God's varied grace: whoever speaks, as one who utters oracles of God; whoever renders service, as one who renders it by the strength which God supplies; in order that in everything God may be glorified through Jesus Christ. To him belong glory and dominion for ever and ever. Amen.

✝ *The Holy Gospel of Our Lord Jesus Christ According to Matthew* [16:24-27]

Jesus told his disciples, "If any man would come after me, let him deny himself and take up his cross and follow me. For whoever would save his life will lose it, and whoever loses his life for my sake will find it. For what will it profit a man, if he gains the whole world and forfeits his life? Or what shall a man give in return for his life? For the Son of man is to come with his angels in the glory of his Father, and then he will repay every man for what he has done."

16. For the Mission of the Church I

A Reading (Lesson) from the Book of Isaiah [2:2-4]

It shall come to pass in the latter days that the mountain of the house of the Lord shall be established as the highest of the mountains, and shall be raised above the hills; and all the nations shall flow to it, and many peoples shall come, and say: "Come, let us go up to the mountain of the Lord, to the house of the God of Jacob; that he may teach us his ways and that we may walk in his paths." For out of Zion shall go forth the law, and the word of the Lord from Jerusalem.

Psalm 96:1-7(8-13) [page 725]

A Reading (Lesson) from the Letter of Paul to the Ephesians [2:13-22]

But now in Christ Jesus you who once were far off have been brought near in the blood of Christ. For he is our peace, who has made us both one, and has broken down the dividing wall of hostility, by abolishing in his flesh the law of commandments and ordinances, that he might create in himself one new man in place of the two, so making peace, and might reconcile us both to God in one body through the cross, thereby bringing the hostility to an end. And he came and preached peace to you who were far off and peace to those who were near; for through him we both have access in one Spirit to the Father. So then you are no longer strangers and sojourners, but you are fellow citizens with the saints and members of the household of God, built upon the foundation of the apostles and prophets, Christ Jesus himself being the cornerstone, in whom the whole structure is joined together and grows into a holy temple in the Lord; in whom you also are built into it for a dwelling place of God in the Spirit.

✝ *The Holy Gospel of Our Lord Jesus Christ According to Luke* [10:1-9]

After this the Lord appointed seventy others, and sent them on ahead of him, two by two, into every town and place where he himself was about to come. And he said to them, "The harvest is plentiful, but the laborers are few; pray therefore the Lord of the harvest to send out laborers into his harvest. Go your way; behold, I send you out as lambs in the midst of wolves. Carry no purse, no bag, no sandals; and salute no one on the road. Whatever house you enter, first say, 'Peace be to this house!' And if a son of peace is there, your peace shall rest upon him; but if not, it shall return to you. And remain in the same house, eating and drinking what they provide, for the laborer deserves his wages; do not go from house to house. Whenever you enter a town and they receive you, eat what is set before you; heal the sick in it and say to them, 'The kingdom of God has come near to you.' "

16. For the Mission of the Church II

A Reading (Lesson) from the Book of Isaiah [49:5-13]

The Lord says, who formed me from the womb to be his servant, to bring Jacob back to him, and that Israel might be gathered to him, for I am honored in the eyes of the Lord, and my God has become my strength — he says: "It is too light a thing that you should be my servant to raise up the tribes of Jacob and to restore the preserved of Israel; I will give you as a light to the nations, that my salvation may reach to the end of the earth." Thus says the Lord, the Redeemer of Israel and his Holy One, to one deeply despised, abhorred by the nations, the servant of rulers: "Kings shall see and arise; princes, and they shall prostrate themselves; because of the Lord, who is faithful, the Holy One of Israel, who has chosen you." Thus says the Lord: "In a time of favor I have answered you, in a day of salvation I have helped you; I have kept you and given you as a covenant to the people, to establish the land, to apportion the desolate heritages; saying to the prisoners, 'Come forth,' to those who are in darkness, 'Appear.' They shall feed along the ways, on all the bare heights shall be their pasture; they shall not hunger or thirst, neither scorching wind nor sun shall smite them, for he who has pity on them will lead them, and by springs of water will guide them. And I will make all my mountains a way, and my highways shall be raised up. Lo, these shall come from afar, and lo, these from the north and from the west, and these from the land of Syene." Sing for joy, O heavens, and exult, O earth; break forth, O mountains, into singing! For the Lord has comforted his people, and will have compassion on his afflicted.

Psalm 67 [page 675]

A Reading (Lesson) from the Letter of Paul to the Ephesians [3:1-12]

For this reason I, Paul, a prisoner for Christ Jesus on behalf of you Gentiles — assuming that you have heard of the stewardship of God's grace that was given to me for you, how the mystery was made known to me by revelation, as I have written briefly. When you read this you can perceive my insight into the mystery of Christ, which was not made known to the sons of men in other generations as it has now been revealed to his holy apostles and prophets by the Spirit; that is, how the Gentiles are fellow heirs, members of the same body and partakers of the promise in Christ Jesus through the gospel. Of this gospel I was made a minister according to the gift of God's grace which was given me by the working of his power. To me, though I am the very least of all the saints, this grace was given, to preach to the Gentiles the unsearchable riches of Christ, and to make all men see what is the plan of the mystery hidden for ages in God who created all things; that through the church the manifold wisdom of God might now be made known to the principalities and powers in the heavenly places. This was according to the eternal purpose which he has realized in Christ Jesus our Lord, in whom we have boldness and confidence of access through our faith in him.

✝ *The Holy Gospel of Our Lord Jesus Christ According to Matthew* [28:16-20]

The eleven disciples went to Galilee, to the mountain to which Jesus had directed them. And when they saw him they worshiped him; but some doubted. And Jesus came and said to them, "All authority in heaven and on earth has been given to me. Go therefore and make disciples of all nations, baptizing them in the name of the Father and of the Son and of the Holy Spirit, teaching them to observe all that I have commanded you; and lo, I am with you always, to the close of the age."

17. For the Nation

[See *Lectionary Texts Year A* (page 261), *Year B* (page 247) and *Year C* (page 255) under "Independence Day July 4," and *Year A* (page 263), *Year B* (page 248) and *Year C* (page 257) under "For the Nation." The Lessons and Psalms may be interchanged.]

18. For Peace

A Reading (Lesson) from the Book of Micah [4:1-5]

It shall come to pass in the latter days that the mountain of the house of the Lord shall be established as the highest of the mountains, and shall be raised up above the hills; and peoples shall flow to it, and many nations shall come, and say: "Come, let us go up to the mountain of the Lord, to the house of the God of Jacob; that he may teach us his ways and we may walk in his paths." For out of Zion shall go forth the law, and the word of the Lord from Jerusalem. He shall judge between many peoples, and shall decide for strong nations afar off; and they shall beat their swords into plowshares, and their spears into pruning hooks; nation shall not lift up sword against nation, neither shall they learn war any more; but they shall sit every man under his vine and under his fig tree, and none shall make them afraid; for the mouth of the Lord of hosts has spoken. For all the peoples walk each in the name of its god, but we will walk in the name of the Lord our God for ever and ever.

Psalm 85:7-13 [page 709]

*A Reading (Lesson) from the Letter of Paul
to the Ephesians* [2:13-18]

But now in Christ Jesus you who once were far off have
been brought near in the blood of Christ. For he is our
peace, who has made us both one, and has broken down
the dividing wall of hostility, by abolishing in his flesh the
law of commandments and ordinances, that he might
create in himself one new man in place of the two, so
making peace, and might reconcile us both to God in one
body through the cross, thereby bringing the hostility to
an end. And he came and preached peace to you who were
far off and peace to those who were near; for through him
we both have access in one Spirit to the Father.

or this

*A Reading (Lesson) from the Letter of Paul
to the Colossians* [3:12-15]

Put on then, as God's chosen ones, holy and beloved,
compassion, kindness, lowliness, meekness, and patience,
forbearing one another and, if one has a complaint against
another, forgiving each other; as the Lord has forgiven
you, so you also must forgive. And above all these put on
love, which binds everything together in perfect harmony.
And let the peace of Christ rule in your hearts, to which
indeed you were called in the one body. And be thankful.

✝ *The Holy Gospel of Our Lord Jesus Christ
According to John* [16:23-33]

Jesus said to his disciples, "In that day you will ask
nothing of me. Truly, truly, I say to you, if you ask
anything of the Father, he will give it to you in my name.
Hitherto you have asked nothing in my name; ask, and
you will receive, that your joy may be full. I have said this

to you in figures; the hour is coming when I shall no longer speak to you in figures but tell you plainly of the Father. In that day you will ask in my name; and I do not say to you that I shall pray the Father for you; for the Father himself loves you, because you have loved me and you believed that I came from the Father. I came from the Father and have come into the world; again, I am leaving the world and going to the Father." His disciples said, "Ah, now you are speaking plainly, not in any figure! Now we know that you know all things, and need none to question you; by this we believe that you came from God." Jesus answered them, "Do you now believe? The hour is coming, indeed it has come, when you will be scattered, every man to his home, and will leave me alone; yet I am not alone, for the Father is with me. I have said this to you, that in me you may have peace. In the world you have tribulation; but be of good cheer, I have overcome the world."

or this

✝ *The Holy Gospel of Our Lord Jesus Christ According to Matthew* [5:43-48]

Jesus said, "You have heard that it was said, 'You shall love your neighbor and hate your enemy.' But I say to you, Love your enemies and pray for those who persecute you, so that you may be sons of your Father who is in heaven; for he makes his sun rise on the evil and on the good, and sends rain on the just and on the unjust. For if you love those who love you, what reward have you? Do not even the tax collectors do the same? And if you salute only your brethren, what more are you doing than others? Do not even the Gentiles do the same? You, therefore, must be perfect, as your heavenly Father is perfect."

19. For Rogation Days

[pages 149-155 above]

20. For the Sick

[page 63 above]

21. For Social Justice

A Reading (Lesson) from the Book of Isaiah [42:1-7]

Behold my servant, whom I uphold, my chosen, in whom my soul delights; I have put my Spirit upon him, he will bring forth justice to the nations. He will not cry or lift up his voice, or make it heard in the street; a bruised reed he will not break, and a dimly burning wick he will not quench; he will faithfully bring forth justice. He will not fail or be discouraged till he has established justice in the earth; and the coastlands wait for his law. Thus says God, the Lord, who created the heavens and stretched them out, who spread forth the earth and what comes from it, who gives breath to the people upon it and spirit to those who walk in it: "I am the Lord, I have called you in righteousness, I have taken you by the hand and kept you; I have given you as a covenant to the people, a light to the nations, to open the eyes that are blind, to bring out the prisoners from the dungeon, from the prison those who sit in darkness."

Psalm 72:1-4(5-11)12-14(15-19) [page 685]

A Reading (Lesson) from the Letter of James
[2:5-9,12-17]

Listen, my beloved brethren. Has not God chosen those
who are poor in the world to be rich in faith and heirs of
the kingdom which he has promised to those who love
him? But you have dishonored the poor man. Is it not the
rich who oppress you, is it not they who drag you into
court? Is it not they who blaspheme the honorable name
which was invoked over you? If you really fulfil the royal
law, according to the scripture, "You shall love your
neighbor as yourself," you do well. But if you show
partiality, you commit sin, and are convicted by the law as
transgressors. So speak and so act as those who are to be
judged under the law of liberty. For judgment is without
mercy to one who has shown no mercy; yet mercy
triumphs over judgment. What does it profit, my brethren,
if a man says he has faith but has not works? Can his faith
save him? If a brother or sister is ill-clad and in lack of
daily food, and one of you says to them, "Go in peace, be
warmed and filled," without giving them the things
needed for the body, what does it profit? So faith by itself,
if it has not works, is dead.

✝ *The Holy Gospel of Our Lord Jesus Christ
According to Matthew* [10:32-42]

Jesus said, "So every one who acknowledges me before
men, I also will acknowledge before my Father who is in
heaven; but whoever denies me before men, I also will
deny before my Father who is in heaven. Do not think that
I have come to bring peace on earth; I have not come to
bring peace, but a sword. For I have come to set a man
against his father, and a daughter against her mother, and
a daughter-in-law against her mother-in-law; and a man's
foes will be those of his own household. He who loves

father or mother more than me is not worthy of me; and he who loves son or daughter more than me is not worthy of me; and he who does not take his cross and follow me is not worthy of me. He who finds his life will lose it, and he who loses his life for my sake will find it. He who receives you receives me, and he who receives me receives him who sent me. He who receives a prophet because he is a prophet shall receive a prophet's reward, and he who receives a righteous man because he is a righteous man shall receive a righteous man's reward. And whoever gives to one of these little ones even a cup of water because he is a disciple, truly, I say to you, he shall not lose his reward."

22. For Social Service

A Reading (Lesson) from the Book of Zechariah
[8:3-12,16-17]

The word of the Lord of hosts came to me, saying, "Thus says the Lord: I will return to Zion, and will dwell in the midst of Jerusalem, and Jerusalem shall be called the faithful city, and the mountain of the Lord of hosts, the holy mountain. Thus says the Lord of hosts: Old men and old women shall again sit in the streets of Jerusalem, each with a staff in hand for very age. And the streets of the city shall be full of boys and girls playing in its streets. Thus says the Lord of hosts: If it is marvelous in the sight of the remnant of this people in these days, should it also be marvelous in my sight, says the Lord of hosts? Thus says the Lord of hosts: Behold, I will save my people from the east country and from the west country; and I will bring them to dwell in the midst of Jerusalem; and they shall be my people and I will be their God, in faithfulness and in righteousness." Thus says the Lord of hosts: "Let your hands be strong, you who in these days have been hearing these words from the mouth of the prophets, since the day that the foundation of the house of the Lord of hosts was laid, that the temple might be built. For before those days there was no wage for man or any wage for beast, neither was there any safety from the foe for him who went out or came in; for I set every man against his fellow. But now I will not deal with the remnant of this people as in the former days, says the Lord of hosts. For there shall be a sowing of peace; the vine shall yield its fruit, and the heavens shall give their dew; and I will cause the remnant of this people to possess all these things. These are the things that you shall do: Speak the truth to one another, render in your gates judgments that are true and make for peace, do not devise evil in your hearts against one another, and love no false oath, for all these things I hate, says the Lord."

Psalm 146 [page 803]   or   *Psalm 22:22-27* [page 611]

A Reading (Lesson) from the First Letter of Peter [4:7-11]

The end of all things is at hand; therefore keep sane and sober for your prayers. Above all hold unfailing your love for one another since love covers a multitude of sins. Practice hospitality ungrudgingly to one another. As each has received a gift, employ it for one another, as good stewards of God's varied grace: whoever speaks, as one who utters oracles of God; whoever renders service, as one who renders it by the strength which God supplies; in order that in everything God may be glorified through Jesus Christ. To him belong glory and dominion for ever and ever. Amen.

✝ *The Holy Gospel of Our Lord Jesus Christ*
According to Mark [10:42-52]

Jesus called the disciples to him and said to them, "You know that those who are supposed to rule over the Gentiles lord it over them, and their great men exercise authority over them. But it shall not be so among you; but whoever would be great among you must be your servant, and whoever would be first among you must be slave of all. For the Son of man also came not to be served but to serve, and to give his life as a ransom for many." And they came to Jericho; and as he was leaving Jericho with his disciples and a great multitude, Bartimae'us, a blind beggar, the son of Timae'us, was sitting by the roadside. And when he heard that it was Jesus of Nazareth, he began to cry out and say, "Jesus, Son of David, have mercy on me!" And many rebuked him, telling him to be silent; but he cried out all the more, "Son of David, have mercy on me!" And Jesus stopped and said, "Call him." And they called the blind man, saying to him, "Take heart; rise, he is calling you." And throwing off his mantle he sprang up and came to Jesus. And Jesus said to him, "What do you want me to do for you?" And the blind man said to him, "Master, let me receive my sight." And Jesus said to him, "Go your way; your faith has made you well." And immediately he received his sight and followed him on his way.

23. For Education

A Reading (Lesson) from the Book of Deuteronomy
[6:4-9,20-25]

Moses said, "Hear, O Israel: The Lord our God is one Lord; and you shall love the Lord your God with all your heart, and with all your soul, and with all your might. And these words which I command you this day shall be upon your heart; and you shall teach them diligently to your children, and shall talk of them when you sit in your house, and when you walk by the way, and when you lie down, and when you rise. And you shall bind them as a sign upon your hand, and they shall be as frontlets between your eyes. And you shall write them on the doorposts of your house and on your gates. When your son asks you in time to come, 'What is the meaning of the testimonies and the statutes and the ordinances which the Lord our God has commanded you?' then you shall say to your son, 'We were Pharaoh's slaves in Egypt; and the Lord brought us out of Egypt with a mighty hand; and the Lord showed signs and wonders, great and grievous, against Egypt and against Pharaoh and all his household, before our eyes; and he brought us out from there, that he might bring us in and give us the land which he swore to give to our fathers. And the Lord commanded us to do all these statutes, to fear the Lord our God, for our good always, that he might preserve us alive, as at this day. And it will be righteousness for us, if we are careful to do all this commandment before the Lord our God, as he has commanded us.' "

Psalm 78:1-7 [page 694]

A Reading (Lesson) from the Second Letter of Paul to Timothy [3:14—4:5]

As for you, continue in what you have learned and have firmly believed, knowing from whom you learned it and how from childhood you have been acquainted with the sacred writings which are able to instruct you for salvation through faith in Christ Jesus. All scripture is inspired by God and profitable for teaching, for reproof, for correction, and for training in righteousness, that the man of God may be complete, equipped for every good work. I charge you in the presence of God and of Christ Jesus who is to judge the living and the dead, and by his appearing and his kingdom: preach the word, be urgent in season and out of season, convince, rebuke, and exhort, be unfailing in patience and in teaching. For the time is coming when people will not endure sound teaching, but having itching ears they will accumulate for themselves teachers to suit their own likings, and will turn away from listening to the truth and wander into myths. As for you, always be steady, endure suffering, do the work of an evangelist, fulfil your ministry.

✠ *The Holy Gospel of Our Lord Jesus Christ According to Matthew* [11:25-30]

Jesus said, "I thank thee, Father, Lord of heaven and earth, that thou hast hidden these things from the wise and understanding and revealed them to babes; yea, Father, for such was thy gracious will. All things have been delivered to me by my Father; and no one knows the Son except the Father, and no one knows the Father except the Son and any one to whom the Son chooses to reveal him. Come to me, all who labor and are heavy laden, and I will give you rest. Take my yoke upon you, and learn from me; for I am gentle and lowly in heart, and you will find rest for your souls. For my yoke is easy, and my burden is light."

24. For Vocation in Daily Work

A Reading (Lesson) from the Book of Ecclesiastes
[3:1,9-13]

For everything there is a season, and a time for every matter under heaven: What gain has the worker from his toil? I have seen the business that God has given to the sons of men to be busy with. He has made everthing beautiful in its time; also he has put eternity into man's mind, yet so that he cannot find out what God has done from the beginning to the end. I know that there is nothing better for them than to be happy and enjoy themselves as long as they live; also that it is God's gift to man that every one should eat and drink and take pleasure in all his toil.

Psalm 8 [page 592]

A Reading (Lesson) from the First Letter of Peter
[2:11-17]

Beloved, I beseech you as aliens and exiles to abstain from the passions of the flesh that wage war against your soul. Maintain good conduct among the Gentiles, so that in case they speak against you as wrongdoers, they may see your good deeds and glorify God on the day of visitation. Be subject for the Lord's sake to every human institution, whether it be to the emperor as supreme, or to governors as sent by him to punish those who do wrong and to praise those who do right. For it is God's will that by doing right you should put to silence the ignorance of foolish men. Live as free men, yet without using your freedom as a pretext for evil; but live as servants of God. Honor all men. Love the brotherhood. Fear God. Honor the emperor.

Matthew 6:19-24 [page 275 below]

25. For Labor Day

A Reading (Lesson) from the Book of Ecclesiasticus
[38:27-32]

So too is every craftsman and master workman who labors by night as well as by day; those who cut the signets of seals, each is diligent in making a great variety; he sets his heart on painting a lifelike image, and he is careful to finish his work. So too is the smith sitting by the anvil, intent upon his handiwork in iron; the breath of the fire melts his flesh, and he wastes away in the heat of the furnace; he inclines his ear to the sound of the hammer, and his eyes are on the pattern of the object. He sets his heart on finishing his handiwork, and he is careful to complete his decoration. So too is the potter sitting at his work and turning the wheel with his feet; he is always deeply concerned over his work, and his output is by number. He molds the clay with his arm and makes it pliable with his feet; he sets his heart to finish the glazing, and he is careful to clean the furnace. All these rely upon their hands, and each is skilful in his own work. Without them a city cannot be established, and men can neither sojourn nor live there.

Psalm 107:1-9 [page 746] or

Psalm 90:1-2,16-17 [page 717]

A Reading (Lesson) from the First Letter of Paul to the Corinthians [3:10-14]

According to the grace of God given to me, like a skilled master builder I laid a foundation, and another man is building upon it. Let each man take care how he builds upon it. For no other foundation can any one lay than that which is laid, which is Jesus Christ. Now if any one builds on the foundation with gold, silver, precious stones, wood, hay, straw—each man's work will become manifest; for the Day will disclose it, because it will be revealed with fire, and the fire will test what sort of work each one has done. If the work which any man has built on the foundation survives, he will receive a reward.

✠ *The Holy Gospel of Our Lord Jesus Christ According to Matthew* [6:19-24]

Jesus said, "Do not lay up for yourselves treasures on earth, where moth and rust consume and where thieves break in and steal, but lay up for yourselves treasure in heaven, where neither moth nor rust consumes and where thieves do not break in and steal. For where your treasure is, there will your heart be also. The eye is the lamp of the body. So, if your eye is sound, your whole body will be full of light; but if your eye is not sound, your whole body will be full of darkness. If then the light in you is darkness, how great is the darkness! No one can serve two masters; for either he will hate the one and love the other, or he will be devoted to the one and despise the other. You cannot serve God and mammon."

Index to Lectionary Texts

Index to Lectionary Texts

What follows is an index of all the citations in the Lectionary from the Book of Common Prayer, 1979, *the* Lesser Feasts and Fasts, *and the* Book of Occasional Services, *arranged in biblical order, together with page references to the full readings as they appear in one or more of the five volumes in the* Lectionary Texts *series. The citations are listed in order from the most inclusive to the least inclusive reading.*

Lectionary Citation	Year A	Year B	Year C	Lesser Feasts & Fasts	Various Occasions & Occasional Services
Genesis					
1:1—2:3	172				
1:1—2:2	110	99	101		
1:26-28					33
2:4-9,15-24					33
2:4b-9,15-25					87
					103
2:4b-9,15-17,25—3:7	51				
2:18-24		197			
3:1-15(16-23)					105
3:1-15(16-22)					88
3:(1-7)8-21		158			
7:1-5,11-18;8:6-18; 9:8-13	112	101	103		
(7:1-5,11-18);8:6-18; 9:8-13					9
					127
8:6-16;9:8-16	140				
8:13-23					142
9:8-17		50			
11:1-9	163	145	151		
12:1-8	53				156
12:1-4a(4b-8)					215
15:1-12,17-18			53		
15:1-6			184		

Lectionary Citation	Year A	Year B	Year C	Lesser Feasts & Fasts	Various Occasions & Occasional Services
Genesis, continued					
17:1-8				69 217	233
18:1-10a(10b-14)			177		
18:1-8					175
18:20-33			179		
22:1-18	94 114	83 103	86 105		
22:1-14		52			
28:10-17	276	261	270		185 247
32:3-8,22-30			208		
37:3-4,12-28				27	
45:3-11,21-28			39		
Exodus					
3:1-15			55		
3:1-12				143	
3:1-6		153			
3:11-15					227
12:1-14a	89	79	81		
14:10—15;1	116	105	107		
14:10-14,21-25; 15:20-21	125				
16:2-4,9-15		177			
16:13-15					43
17:1-7	56			34	
19:1-9a,16-20a; 20:18-20	164	146	152		11
19:2-8a	179				
19:3-8					257
20:1-17		54			
22:21-27	217				
23:9-16,20-21					118
24:12(13-14)15-18	45				

Lectionary Citation	Year A	Year B	Year C	Lesser Feasts & Fasts	Various Occasions & Occasional Services
Nehemiah					
8:1-4a,5-6,8					180
8:2-10			30		
9:6-15	148				
9:16-20	193				
Esther					
14:1-6,12-14				17	
Job					
4:12-21					171
14:1-14	107	96	98		
19:21-27a					67
19:23-27a			215		
38:1-11,16-18		163			153
42:1-6			128		
Proverbs					
2:1-9				214	
3:1-7				208	
				288	
3:1-6	274	259	268		
4:10-18				223	
9:1-6		181			
31:10-11,20,26,28				263	
Ecclesiastes					
1:12-14;2:(1-7,11) 18-23			182		
3:1-15					120
3:1-11					81
3:1,9-13					273
12:1-8					121
12:1-7					82

Lectionary Citation	Year A	Year B	Year C	Lesser Feasts & Fasts	Various Occasions & Occasional Services
Isaiah, continued					
52:13-15;53:10-12					239
53:3-5					47
53:4-12		201			
55:1-13					249
55:1-11	118	107	109		13
					133
55:1-5,10-13	187				
55:6-11				15	
56:1(2-5)6-7	197				
57:14b-21		172			
58:1-12	48	47	47		
58:1-9a				10	
58:6-12				259	
58:9b-14				12	
59:(1-4)9-19		203			
60:1-6,9	26	25	24		
61:1-9					25
					135
61:1-8					189
61:1-4				156	
61:1-3					47
					66
					228
61:10—62:3	19	19	18		
61:10-11	270	255	264		
62:1-5			28		
62:6-7,10-12	15	15	14		
64:1-9a		5			92
65:17-25		9		44	98
66:10-16			172		

Lectionary Citation	Year A	Year B	Year C	Lesser Feasts & Fasts	Various Occasions & Occasional Services
Jeremiah					
1:4-10			33	150 215	
1:4-9					201
3:21—4:2		32			
7:1-7(8-15)			42		
7:23-28				40	
11:18-20				55	
14:(1-6)7-10,19-22			210		
14:1-9					150
15:15-21	200			277	
17:5-10			37	26	
17:7-8					241
18:1-11,18-20				24	
20:7-13	181			70	
23:1-6			219		
23:23-29			187		
26:1-9,12-15	231	218	225		
31:7-14	23	23	21		
31:15-17	235	222	229		
31:31-34		59			26 91
32:36-41			132		
45:1-5	266	252	260		
Lamentations					
3:22-26,31-33					66
Ezekiel					
1:3-5a,15-22,26-28		140			
2:1-7		168			
11:17-20	169				
18:1-4,25-32	209				
18:21-28				19	
31:1-6,10-14		161			

Lectionary Citation	Year A	Year B	Year C	Lesser Feasts & Fasts	Various Occasions & Occasional Services
Ecclesiasticus					
2:(1-6)7-11	285	270	279		
2:7-11,16-18				138	
2:7-11				296	
10:(7-11)12-18			191		
15:11-20	38				
27:30—28:7	204				
38:1-4,6-10,12-14	277	262	271		
38:27-32					152
					274
39:1-10				229	
39:1-9				196	
				242	
39:1-8					201
43:1-22					121
44:1-10,13-14	283	267	277		163
44:1-7				195	
47:8-10				169	
51:1-12				275	
Baruch					
4:36—5:9					95
5:1-9			6		
Song of the Three Young Men					
2-4,11-20a				37	
Susanna					
1-9,15-29,34-62				56	
41-62				60	
1 Maccabees					
2:49-64					159
2 Maccabees					
6:1-2;7:1-23					160

Lectionary Citation	Year A	Year B	Year C	Lesser Feasts & Fasts	Various Occasions & Occasional Services
Mark, continued					
14:3-9	83	72	74		
14:32—15:39(40-47)		63			
15:1-39(40-47)		66			
15:40-47		70			
16:1-8		114			
16:9-15,19-20	159	142	147		
16:9-15,20	139	124	127		
16:15-20	251	236	245	158	
Luke					
1:5-25					99
1:26-58					109
1:26-38(39-56)					100
1:26-38	248	13 234	242		
1:26-33(34-38)					235
1:26-33				218	
1:39-49(50-56)			11		
1:39-46(47-56)					111
1:39-49	254	239	248		
1:46-55	271	256	265		
1:57-80	258	244	252		112
2:1-20					114
2:1-14(15-20)	13	14	13		
2:(1-14)15-20	15	16	15		
2:15-21	22	22	21		
2:21-36					115
2:22-40	241	228	235		
2:41-52	25 246	25 232	23 240		
2:41-51					42
3:1-6			8		
3:7-18			9		
3:15-16,21-22			28		140

Lectionary Citation	Year A	Year B	Year C	Lesser Feasts & Fasts	Various Occasions & Occasional Services
John, continued					
5:19-24				166	
				179	
5:24-27				136	73
					80
5:30-47				52	
6:1-15				83	
6:(1-7)8-13					184
6:4-15		58			
6:16-21				84	
6:22-29				85	
6:24-35		178			
6:30-35				87	
6:35-40				88	
6:35-38					200
6:37-51		180			
6:37-40					73
6:44-51				91	
6:47-58					238
6:47-51					60
6:52-59				94	
6:53-59		182			
6:57-63				137	
6:60-69		184		96	
7:1-2,10,25-30				54	
7:16-18				225	
7:37-52				55	
7:37-39a	168	150	156		
8:1-11				61	
8:12-20				62	
8:21-30				66	
8:25-32				194	
8:31-42				68	
8:51-59				70	
9:1-13(14-27)28-38	62			46	

Lectionary Citation	Year A	Year B	Year C	Lesser Feasts & Fasts	Various Occasions & Occasional Services
Romans, continued					
7:21—8:6	186				
8:9-17	188				
8:12-17		154			
8:14-19,34-35,37-39					68
8:14-17,22-27	168	149	155		
8:14-17					16
8:18-27					28
8:18-25	190				151
8:18-23					51
8:26-34	192				
8:31-39		53			51
8:35-39	194			251	83
9:1-5	196				
10:(5-8a)8b-13			51		
10:8b-18	228	215	222		
10:8b-17				260	
10:13-17				225	
11:13-15,29-32	198				
11:33-36	199				228
12:1-18					206
12:1-8	201				28
12:6-12					181
12:9-21	203			177	
12:9-13				220	
13:1-10	263	249	257		
13:8-14	5				
14:5-12	205				
14:7-9,10b-12				227	
15:4-13	7				
16:25-27		12			
1 Corinthians					
1:1-9	30	6			
1:10-17	32				

Lectionary Citation	Year A	Year B	Year C	Lesser Feasts & Fasts	Various Occasions & Occasional Services
1 Corinthians, continued					
1:18-31	84	74	76		
1:(18-25)26-31	34				
1:18-25				202	
1:18-24					240
1:22-31					219
1:26-31				297	
2:1-11	37				
2:6-13				209	
2:6-10,13-16				255 286	
3:1-11,16-17					212
3:1-9	39				
3:4-11				180	
3:5-11				288	254
3:8-11				197	
3:9-14				249	
3:10-14					152 275
3:10-11,16-23	41				
3:11-23				206	
4:1-5(6-7)8-13	43				
4:9-15	272	257	266		
5:6b-8	129	115	117		
6:11b-20		30			
7:17-23		32			
8:1b-13		34			
9:16-23		37		233	
9:24-27		40			
10:1-13			57		
10:1-4,16-17					237
11:23-26(27-32)	90	80	82		
11:23-29					238
12:1-11			29		

Lectionary Citation	Year A	Year B	Year C	Lesser Feasts & Fasts	Various Occasions & Occasional Services
2 Thessalonians					
1:1-5(6-10)11-12			213		
2:13—3:5			215		
3:6-13			217		
1 Timothy					
1:12-17			197		
2:1-8			199		
2:1-7a				243	
3:1-7					193
3:8-13					203
3:14-16					234
6:7-10,17-19					154
6:11-19			201		
2 Timothy					
1:(1-5)6-14			204		
1:1-8				149	
1:6-14				258	
1:11-14				228	
2:1-7				268	
2:1-5,10				240	
2:(3-7)8-15			207		
2:10-15,19				173	
2:22b-26				213	
3:14—4:5			209		272
3:14-17	275	260	269	244	
4:1-8	260	246	254		
4:5-13	278	263	272		
4:6-8,16-18			211		
Titus					
1:1-5				149	
2:7-8,11-14				264	
2:11-14	13	14	13		
3:4-7	15	16	14		